THE UNION OF 1707

THE UNION OF 1707

ITS IMPACT ON SCOTLAND

Essays by

P W J Riley
A L Murray
R H Campbell
A Fenton
I S Ross and
S A C Scobie

Edited by

T I Rae

BLACKIE & SON LIMITED
1974

Blackie and Son Limited
Bishopbriggs, Glasgow G64 2NZ
5 Fitzhardinge Street, London W1H 0DL

First published 1974
© The contributors 1974

Printed in Great Britain.
Printed by Econoprint Ltd., Edinburgh.

Contents

Preface

The five essays in this volume were first delivered as lectures at the Sixth Scottish Historical Conference held at the University of Stirling in September 1972. The theme, 'The Impact of Union', chosen by the conference organisers for this occasion, was intended 'to distinguish some of the intricately-woven threads that comprise the web of that complex entity, modern Scotland', by examining how the Union of 1707 'affected the Scottish people at various levels of their existence'. Politics, administration, agriculture, industry and literature were among the topics chosen for elucidation.

The perhaps over-pompously expressed intention may not have been entirely fulfilled, for in the course of a two-day conference the complexities of such a vast subject can only be outlined. The speakers, working completely independently, were very much in agreement in suggesting that in many respects the impact of Union was less than has popularly been supposed. Post-Union changes in Scotland often followed trends and tendencies which were already in evidence in the seventeenth century; the abilities and character of Scotsmen continued to develop Scotland's potential in many spheres almost uninfluenced by the English connection. Even in politics and administration, where the link caused the major changes, Scottish institutions retained their character and individuality.

This emphasis on continuity after 1707 does by no means make up the complete picture; yet it is an aspect of the growth of Scotland which cannot be ignored at the present day. The conference organisers felt that the viewpoint was worthy of a wider and larger audience than that which attended the conference; we hope that these essays will be of interest to all Scots wherever they may be.

T.I. RAE   Edinburgh
Scottish Historical Conference Trust   August 1973

vii

The structure of Scottish politics and the Union of 1707

P W J RILEY BA PhD

Lecturer in History, University of Manchester

Whatever else they had on their minds between the revolution of 1688 and the Union there was one problem of great concern to many Englishmen and to some Scotsmen: that of governing Scotland within the framework of the union of the crowns. It was a consequence of trying to run the two Kingdoms in harness, given the structure of Scottish politics and the impact upon it of the English political situation. In times of crisis the problem always became more pressing and after 1688 increasingly so. To some extent — exactly how far is a matter of opinion — the Union was an attempt to escape its complications.

From the point of view of a Scottish political manager and his, for the most part English, masters, the main task of government was that of handling the Scottish parliament. A court party had to be constructed which was large enough to dominate it. There were obstacles in plenty to achieving this, ranging from travelling difficulties on the Great North Road to Scotland's political dependence on her neighbouring kingdom; in relation to the Union and its consequences two were especially significant. The great interests in Scottish politics were virtually impossible to cope with in a separate kingdom and this was especially so after 1689 when the Scottish parliament emerged as a force to be reckoned with. There were hazards too in the very different party structures which existed in Scotland and England.

'Overmighty subjects' had been a fact of political life in both kingdoms. They were slower to disappear in Scotland than in England. By the end of the seventeenth century threats from overmighty subjects in England were over. If

1

Thomas Pelham-Holles, Duke of Newcastle, is exluded —
usually quoted as an example but really an exception —
power had come to be based on favour and ability.
Sunderland had depended on favour and his wits, Rochester
was one of the family, Godolphin had progressed through
competent administration, Marlborough through military
prowess and the favour of Queen Anne. The rest, the lords of
the junto, Harley, Walpole, had come up the hard way, owing
what success they had to some combination of favour, ability
and persistence. The real territorial magnates had for the
most part no ambition to wield power at the centre. They
were interested in local influence and, from the crown, places
of dignity and profit rather than power. Such were
Devonshire, who served William and Anne, content with the
consolidation of his territorial interest and the post of Lord
Steward, and John, Earl of Clare and later, through
importunity, Duke of Newcastle, having married the daughter
and heiress of the last Cavendish Newcastle. The latter's chief
ambition was to re-establish the Cavendish northern empire
at the expense of Devonshire and his other neighbours. His
parliamentary influence was extensive but he did not seem to
worry overmuch about the behaviour of the nine or so M.P.s
whose election he secured. In the central government he held
no more than the Privy Seal's place which he seems to have
enjoyed from Welbeck Abbey. What he really coveted was
the post of Justiciar North of the Trent. In 1710 he tried to
make his support for Harley conditional on his being given
this post in perpetuity but accepted a life grant and until he
died in 1711 gave his alliance to Harley. This Duke of
Newcastle was typical of the English magnates.[1]

Scottish magnates were very different. They were
obsessed with central power to an extent which seemed in
the late seventeenth century to increase rather than diminish.
Their earlier capacity for causing trouble needs no
elaboration, but the circumstances of 1688–9, the
consequent political and religious settlements together with
the accident of personality made the problem of the Scottish
magnates critical. A few powerful nobles vacated the political
scene at the revolution on account of their adherence to

2

popery, jacobitism or both, but some very restless personalities were left. By the Union there were the four dukes who could properly be described as magnates: Hamilton, Queensberry, Atholl and Argyll. They and their fathers had been in competition before and since the revolution. The trouble was that each of them wanted not only power in the government but a monopoly of power. To obtain this each of them demonstrated amply that he would embrace any policy and almost any cause, stopping at little: misrepresentation, conspiracy, character-assassination, double-dealing and, in at least one instance, forgery.

There were, in addition, lesser men who retained a belief in the possibility of founding magnate interests and the hope that they might be the ones to succeed. In the recent past what could be done had been shown by William, first Duke of Queensberry who, through royal favour and long tenure of office, had made a fortune. The examples of Lauderdale and the Drummonds were not so encouraging but this could always be put down to misfortune or miscalculation. Lord Melville, the Dalrymples and Annandale amongst others still lived in the hope of founding powerful interests; their efforts to do so produced one intolerable situation after another.

This was the state of affairs in which Scotland had to be managed. After 1689 there was a Scottish parliament free to function as an institution in its own right instead of being the largely formal body of an earlier time. It had become, though, a prey to rivalries between magnates and those aspiring to be such. Alliances were formed quickly in opposition; court coalitions were not only precarious but for the most part impracticable.

Throughout William's reign various methods of managing Scotland had been used with a notable lack of success. At the beginning of the reign William had tried to employ the third Duke of Hamilton without alienating Queensberry, Atholl and Argyll, the idea being to use Hamilton without giving him the monopoly of power for which he craved. In the event this annoyed Argyll and confirmed Queensberry and Atholl in their resolution to trifle even further with jacobitism without in any way satisfying Hamilton; his reaction was to make things intolerable for the court. Whether in favour or out of it he wanted full control of the administration and his demands were incessant. In the spring of 1694, James 'Secretary' Johnston, after suffering a barrage of demands and complaints, announced that he would rather be a porter than spend another such winter with Hamilton.[2]

In an attempt to avoid the problem, government by non-magnate interests was adopted for a period with merely token recognition for the magnate families. Management was put in the hands of Melville, the Dalrymples, Tweeddale and Johnston. All fought amongst themselves to increase their power, and what had been overlooked was the fact that the only thing certain to produce an alliance amongst the magnates was the belief that they were being collectively slighted. Hamilton died in 1694, but Queensberry and his eldest son, Drumlanrig, Atholl and his eldest son, soon to be Earl of Tullibardine, and Argyll, intrigued incessantly against these non-magnate ministries.

By 1696 the government of Scotland had reached the point of collapse. William succumbed to pressure from what was referred to as 'the nobility of the first rank', to reconstruct the ministry and give territorial power and prestige its due weight in the government. The assumption was made that since these magnates had been united in opposition they would continue to be allied in a coalition ministry. It proved to be ill-founded. The court party was turned into a bird bath. Atholl's interest was represented by Tullibardine as Secretary. Argyll was in, tirelessly denouncing Tullibardine as a jacobite and sham presbyterian. The second Duke of Queensberry, formerly Drumlanrig and recently succeeded to his father's title, was Lord Privy Seal and jealous of everybody. On one thing only were they all agreed: no nonsense was to be taken from lesser beings. Sir James Ogilvy, later Earl of Seafield, had been appointed jointly Secretary of State with Tullibardine. The latter told him he was not expected to interfere in anything. Marchmont, the Lord Chancellor, was ordered to conduct himself with respect towards his betters and he promised to do so.[3] The

4

administration seethed with internal jealousy and dissatisfaction.

The subsequent battle to dominate the ministry saw
Tullibardine forced out; this left as the main court interests
Queensberry and Argyll who, largely as a consequence of the
personality of Archibald, first Duke of Argyll, collaborated
for a time better than most. But over the next few years the
magnate problem became personified by Queensberry. From
1696 the duke worked steadily with all the political weapons
at his disposal to turn the court interest into his own personal
following. In the process he showed, for the sake of his own
ambition, a complete disregard of what should have been his
main task — that of managing parliament. By the end of
William's reign his attitude had rent the ministry by
antagonising Argyll; more significantly Queensberry's behaviour had also alarmed the king who was being placed in
a serious predicament. As things were, the session of
parliament proposed for 1702 could not be managed without
Queensberry, but if Queensberry was allowed to transform
the court interest into his own it could not be managed with
him either. Anne's ministry faced the same difficulty
between 1703 and 1705. Just before his death William gave
the impression of being in full retreat from all decisions
connected with Scottish politics. There was some excuse for
this in that almost any decision relating to Scotland was
likely to create more problems than it solved. From this time
until the Union Queensberry epitomised the position of the
magnate in Scotland.

This incompatibility of magnate interests was bad
enough. It was made a more intractable problem in that it cut
right across what was taken to be a main consideration of
Scottish management. The argument was repeatedly
advanced that Scotland could not be ruled by coalitions or
'motley ministries' which encouraged only restlessness,
intrigue and opposition. The kingdom could be managed,
according to this contention, only by a court that was 'all of
a piece' — one unified interest, a magnate fully backed, and
seen to be so, by the dominant interest at the English court.
The goal of management was thought to be the building up

of one such interest to a point at which all others had to accept it as the dominant power in Scotland and come to terms with it. Naturally this was an argument which greatly commended itself to those who hoped to secure the removal of rivals from the ministry and themselves to comprise this dominant interest. In 1705–6, during the argument about the choice of Union Commissioners, this point of view was given full expression by a Queensberry source; the persons nominated should be 'all of a piece'.

'. . . whatever may be pretended that it is fit for effectuating the design to engage all parties in the treaty [of union] this is certain, that if any is named who are not united and in good correspondence with the queen's servants nor will not make application to them to be named but set up for themselves, independent of the ministry, such persons will never be cordial in advancing the queen's service in this ministry's hands, and if they can have the interest to be named against the ministry's will or without their consent this must infallibly encourage them and others to join with them in opposition to the present ministry.

'The differences amongst the queen's servants and those employed and trusted by her have been the great occasion that hath retarded and embarrassed the public service . . . opposition will fall off and dwindle if the servants are encouraged and supported and all the world sees the queen puts active confidence in them and will employ and trust none in her service but whom they recommend. But if others are put upon them who are known not to be in friendship with them it will still be thought these others have more interest and esteem at court than the servants and this must inevitably weaken the influence of the servants and encourage opposers. . . .'[4]

This was a plain statement and, partial or not, it contained an element of truth or, at least, since no other system worked this was the only one with possibilities. There had to be no hope for dissident elements of either prevailing with the sovereign or of being pulled in the wake of an advancing English faction. The danger of oppositions being encouraged was very great under William and Anne. Scotland was low in William's scale of priorities and the kingdom was a nuisance to him. Its nuisance value was due not only to the behaviour of the magnates but also to his precarious position in English politics. His attempts to create balanced ministries led to internal power struggles; his foreign policy, especially after the peace of 1697, led to a thriving opposition. Both were complications which provided dissident Scots with possible ladders to influence. The political situation in England, particularly in view of the party structure, was always such that some were prepared to encourage opposition in Scotland — over Darien, over the 1702 parliament, over religion — to embarrass the court. So it was possible to acquire political credit in Scotland by carrying some rumour from London, or showing a letter from some English politician, seeming to indicate that the English court was on the brink of radical changes as a consequence of which the situation in Scotland was likely to take a different turn. Such rumour-mongering was a standard tactic in Anglo-Scottish politics.[5]

The Scottish magnates and their followers, whether in or out, were completely devoid of any sense of responsibility for anything but their own prospects. Regardless of the needs of Scotland, of the crown, or of anything else, they followed their own interest with single-minded devotion. In some instances the cause lay in extensive debts. Even if they thought much about principles, some were quite unable to afford them. But more than that was involved. Next to no responsibility for Scotland's fate rested in Scotland. The kingdom was politically subordinate to England and it was there that the decisions were made. As a result Scottish politicians played the system for what it was worth and made what they could out of it. The government was looked upon as an institution to be exploited. Without qualms the greater nobles would undertake to carry a policy they had no affection for and knowing it had no hope of success. At least it gave them an office and a salary; when they failed they could put the blame on someone else and still have a chance of being left in their jobs whether or not anyone believed them.

7

So the seemingly ideal method of managing Scotland was not one which could be easily adopted. All the crown could do in the main was to suffer what happened and try to ameliorate its effects, however slightly, by such schemes as seemed feasible and quite a few that did not: the magnate coalition of 1696, for instance, the cavalier alliance of 1703 and the new party experiment of 1704, none of which suceeded.

Obviously for the sake of management the power of the magnates had to be reduced. It had to be beyond the power of a Queensberry to hold the court to ransom. Given the increased power of the Scottish parliament and the entrenched positions of the high nobility it is difficult to see how this problem could have been solved other than by a union and a united kingdom within which the Scottish nobles would be less formidable. The state of Scotland was fully appreciated at the time. As one pamphleteer put it in 1703:

'The animosities between two eminent families there [in Scotland] does certainly very much straiten the queen's choice at present; for betwixt these two, the nation is so distracted into parties, that if her majesty is influenced in her choice of ministry by either of them, she must henceforward resolve to manage herself by the unruly and unstable measures of faction. . . .'[6]

In court circles the need for cutting down the 'insolence of the boisterous pretending grandees'[7] was recognised as urgent. It was notorious enough to be referred to in one of Lord Belhaven's remarkable speeches:

'. . . there has got up a kind of aristocracy . . . a kind of undertakers and pragmatic statesmen, who finding their power and strength great and answerable to their designs, will make bargains with our gracious sovereign; they will serve her faithfully, but upon their own terms; they must have their own instruments, their own measures; this man must be turned out, and that man put in, and then they'll make her the most glorious queen in Europe . . . .'[8]

Belhaven at the time was using this argument, somewhat obscurely, to oppose union. Others recognised union as the only feasible solution. There is little doubt that the noises favourable to union which the court began to emit at the end of William's reign were designed to rid the king of an embarrassing situation in Scotland, as well as to strengthen the court at Westminster. Anne's court managers inherited this policy and pursued it for the same reasons. Certainly by 1706 Godolphin and the queen had had their fill of Queensberry, Argyll and Hamilton and privately said so. The need for union was accepted by a scattered group of Scots who had been intimately acquainted with the task of governing Scotland within the union of crowns. Their convictions were to some extent academic in that they were overlaid by the day-to-day exigencies of politics but they were nonetheless real. All of them had experienced the difficulties of managing Scottish magnates and the complications introduced by the needs of English politics. They included the first Earl of Stair, Seafield and, in his more philosophical moments, Cromartie. They were part of an influential nucleus of opinion that union was the only way to tame the factions which made Scotland ungovernable. And when such men spoke of faction they knew what they were talking about. The magnates were going to have to be disciplined and their ambitions curtailed to the level of the English dukes.

Before examining whether union had this desired effect let us for a moment consider the difficulties caused by the differing structure of parties in the two kingdoms. In England, over a period from the exclusion crisis of 1679—81 through the revolution to the crucial year of 1696, the structure of political parties had changed from the court-country distinction of Charles II's reign to the more rigid division between whig and tory. With few exceptions and those quite explicable, voting in England was on party lines. One of the basic causes of the rigid party split was undoubtedly the phenomenon of junto ambition together with their cohesion and organisation allied to a certain exclusiveness, all of which produced a paler reflection of these attributes amongst the tories. The parties had official ideologies, largely historical survivals, which some at grass

roots level actually believed in but which were in practice
frequently ignored by the leaders. Party discipline,
considering the difficulties the managers had to contend
with, was surprisingly tight. So, although it was possible for
people to change sides — some of them did — it was rare for
them to change back again. Permanent courtiers were few.
Aside from the personal following of the court managers for
the time being there was a mere handful of civil servants who,
whatever their private opinions, voted by convention with the
court and a few 'poor lords' who lacked the means to
maintain their dignity without court supplements to their
incomes. In return they did as they were told and were often
ashamed of it.[9]

In Scotland, by contrast, the pattern remained very
much one of 'ins' and 'outs' whatever justifications were
made for opposition. The so-called 'country' opposition,
concerned vocally for the interests of the nation, was
composed of successive strata of those excluded from the
court: the Tweeddale, Atholl and Hamilton interests.
Nobody at the time entertained any illusions about the
motives of the opposition although the Darien business gave
them a magnificent opportunity to pose as patriots. In 1703
this 'country' party had been joined by the cavaliers, eager to
support the court until their hopes of advancement were
disappointed after which they began to talk of patriotism. In
behaviour there was little difference between Hamilton out
all the time, Tweeddale and Atholl most of the time and
Queensberry out in 1704—5. It was all remarkably like the
England of Charles II — a court-country division but with
internal court rivalries which occasionally allied some of the
courtiers with the country opposition to undermine their
opponents in the ministry. None of this is to deny that some
people felt strongly about some things: Fletcher in the
opposition and Cockburn of Ormiston in the ministry, both
being 'loners', independent, irascible and arrogant. Such men
were few. The rest comprised the magnates, a law unto
themselves, men with encumbered estates anxious to
supplement their rents preferably with something regular
which carried perquisites rather than a salary or pension which

was never paid, career men, lawyers mostly, aspiring to be judges or clerks of parliament or session, usually to be found in the following of some magnate in the hope sooner or later of attaining their goal. Sheer poverty and the need for legal protection in a kingdom where legal process was bound up with politics made patronage of incomparably greater importance in Scotland than in England. The result was a large body of court supporters who would come to terms with anyone rather than be out in the cold, for only the magnates and their followers could afford to be on the outside for long and they were gambling on their nuisance value.

This difference between the party structures of the two kingdoms had been an additional source of trouble, less obvious than magnate rivalries but quite serious especially since it involved religion. The issue of the Scottish religious settlement had played a key part in politics not so much through religious conviction as by reason of the connection between England and Scotland. A fact tacitly accepted by post-revolution governments in Scotland was that politically, all professions to the contrary notwithstanding, there was no real alternative to some form of presbyterian establishment. A hard core on each side was for various reasons including religious conviction firmly against all compromise. The government's choice had to be dictated by political necessity and the circumstances of 1689–90 led to presbyterianism. A direct result was that zealous episcopalianism became, not unjustifiably, equated with jacobitism. Subsequently all ministries seem to have drawn the conclusion that the situation was better left alone.

However, the English connection entangled religion and politics to an even greater extent. A standard device of Scots trying to improve their position was to tout for English tory support by posing as champions of downtrodden epis-copalianism – those who were, as Sir George Mackenzie would have had Nottingham believe, 'of the Church of England persuasion'.[10] The tactic had been used by sucessive waves of opposition. Those trying to gain influence affected to stand for a square deal for episcopalians against the

11

severity of a high presbyterian ministry. Once in office, if their manoeuvre was successful, they could do little or nothing about it and left things as they were only to be stigmatised in their turn as 'bigots' and 'hot men'. It was all talk and amongst Scottish politicians it gave rise to few illusions. Those who were misled were English tories: Leeds, Nottingham and Normanby.

The outcome was the confusion inevitable when large numbers of people are acting under a misapprehension. English tories assumed too readily, because of their own party structure, that Scots professing episcopalian sympathies were Scottish tories. The junto made a similar assumption about professed presbyterians; they took them to be good whigs. It was some time before either party became enlightened. Queensberry, for instance, entered the Scottish ministry in any significant capacity first of all in 1696 as a member of an episcopalian family with a following of episcopalians. In England he was looked on by both parties as a Scottish tory. Yet no changes in the religious settlement were made or even contemplated under Queensberry's auspices. By 1702 some of the Scottish opposition began to represent their struggle as being, amongst other things, one against a gang of intolerant presbyterians led by Queensberry. One of the duke's political triumphs was his success in persuading Anne's tory ministry that he was really an episcopalian hamstrung by a crowd of presbyterian fanatics. But when, during the parliamentary session of 1703, things went awry, he chose to play for safety, supporting the presbyterians and babbling of jacobite plots. Suddenly the junto began to see him as a good Scottish whig, the 'proto-rebel' and their hope for Scotland. The fact was that at this stage the Scots did not fit into English categories and the English had difficulty in envisaging any other category to fit them in to. It is not surprising that the English for much of the time regarded Scottish politics with bewilderment and impatience.

If one asks how this situation was affected by the Union two main questions need to be answered. First of all how far was the Scottish party structure affected by contact with the more rigid English system? And, secondly, how far was the power of the magnates reduced to tolerable proportions?

The firm two-party structure of Anne's reign did not last for any length of time but there are signs that the Scots were slowly accommodating themselves to it and would in time have been absorbed into the two-party division. It was certainly not an immediate effect of the Union. Having accepted Queensberry and his following as good whigs the junto backed them right up to 1707 hoping that Scotland's representation would be made up of the Queensberry group which would change the party balance at Westminster in the whigs' favour. All this indicates a certain blindness on the part of the junto. Queensberry was not a whig in anybody's terms — he was a magnate and did what seemed best for himself. Not surprisingly, the Scottish court proved, at Westminster, to be courtiers and added to the court's strength against the junto, a development which acutely distressed the whig lords. They began to pose as men who had tried valiantly to do Godolphin a good turn and who for their pains had been spurned when he found new friends.

The junto were despondent but not passive. To harass and weaken the English court and undermine the Scottish court party before the 1708 elections they joined, in the session of 1707–8, with the squadrone to force the abolition of the Scottish privy council, looked on as the core of the court party's influence. Much to the court's discomfiture they succeeded. But, it is worth noting, they were joined by the squadrone, formerly allies of Godolphin and Harley and but recently stigmatised by the junto as jacobites. And the squadrone were deserting Godolphin to pay off old scores against Queensberry and John, second Duke of Argyll. Argyll's political assassination of the squadrone in 1705 had created bad blood which was not to fade till the late 1730s when, for one reason or another, they found themselves on the same side. To further confuse the pattern the whigs were joined in 1708 by Hamilton and the Scottish jacobites. Clearly the Scots had not yet received the imprint of the English political pattern, whilst the English were tending to take the Scots as they found them.

Two developments seemed, in time, to make a difference. There was the success of the junto in the English elections of 1708 which left Godolphin and the English court little alternative to being whig allies. Later, there was the tory victory of 1710 which, aided by whig propaganda, produced clear-cut issues, delicate enough in England but in Scotland very sensitive: the Scottish religious settlement and the succession.

After 1708 the Scottish courtiers stayed with Godolphin in his enforced capitulation to junto pressure and for the most part fought the 1710 election as whigs. There was even some competition amongst the Scots to demonstrate how much better whigs they were than other people. This produced some unusual alliances. A collaboration between Leven and Rothes in Fife was not far removed from being a sign of the end of the world, but it happened. It seems that the party system at Westminster was beginning to push the Scots into the same mould. The process, though, was still far from complete. To the Scots, English whigs and tories were alien categories only to be used, not accepted. Defections from the Scottish court played no small part in Harley's scheme of 1710: Argyll, Mar, Wemyss, Northesk, all joined the anti-Queensberry interests of Hamilton and Annandale. This was a reproduction of the old pattern — a group forming against the interest which seemed to be running Scotland. It was no accident that the Harleyite coalition comprised all the excluded magnates: Hamilton and Atholl as well as Argyll and his brother, Islay. This was very much like old times.

Also in the old style was the behaviour of Queensberry. The events of 1710 presented him with embarrassing dilemmas. His following had splintered and future developments seemed uncertain. He fell back on the old magnate tactics — kept his head down, did nothing overtly, made encouraging noises to both sides and hoped for the best. The time for this was past and Queensberry proved to be a casualty. After the tory election victory in 1710 he kept his job as Secretary but only because it relieved Harley of the problems which would have arisen through his dismissal.

The tory landslide of 1710 was an embarrassment to Harley, bringing him some supporters he would rather have done without. His ability to control events and intervene in elections was limited by the fact that he was trying to look as if he were going one way whilst in fact standing still. He really wanted a mixed and moderate court party in Scotland. Under the circumstances this was not feasible and it was in the commons elections that the lack of control showed when they produced amongst the twenty-odd supporters of the court a crop of cavaliers, bringing them for the first time since the Union boldly into the political scene. There was a period of quiescence whilst the cavaliers were allowed to hope without anything actually being done for them. Baillie could remain at the Board of Trade, Leven and Glasgow could make professions of loyalty to Harley and the queen's service and keep their jobs and even the squadrone could indicate their willingness to run Scotland for Harley if called on to do so.

What finally produced an English-style polarisation between Scottish groups was the breakdown of Harley's policy of moderation and non-committal behaviour. Changes were made which, to Scotsmen with convictions or fears for their own interest, meant either jacobitism rampant, an episcopalian restoration or both. A pressure group of Scottish cavaliers succeeded in securing the passage of the Toleration Act of 1712 and the acts restoring patronages and the 'yule vacance'. These measures were accompanied by changes in office which always had a disturbing effect on people's outlook. Fence-sitters had to decide how to come down. The consequence was that between 1712 and 1714 Scottish representation divided with increasing sharpness between court and opposition, a split which inevitably corresponded with whig and tory in England. Some of this was due to conviction, some to resentment, but a contributory factor was that at Westminster it was increasingly apparent to the Scots that one was expected to choose one side or the other and when the choice had been made the English parties exerted organisational pressure to make it virtually binding.

By the death of Anne and the Hanoverian succession English habits and convention had had enough effect to leave some lingering cohesion amongst the Scottish groups. The former opposition to the tory court naturally claimed their reward although they were divided between the old Scottish court group now supporting Argyll, and the squadrone. The change appears in the behaviour of the supporters of Anne's last ministry. Seafield,[11] who by this time regarded himself as being above party politics and who had been employed by Oxford[12] because he was able, did not expect to keep his job. Nor did he, but he was unusual in making it perfectly clear that he supported the court whoever it was. Others who had joined the tory administration as courtiers rather than as tories seemed to have come to look on themselves as a Scottish tory interest and were prepared to hang together even in defeat and attempt to make their own terms with the new king if terms were to be made. There was some competition for the leadership of a Scottish tory interest even in eclipse, one of the contenders being Mar.[13] John Pringle of Haining wrote to tell Sir John Clerk that he thought it for his own good to remain with the interest with which he had been recently engaged even though they were out of favour.[14] Whilst old habits died hard and magnates acted as they had always acted, a process had been under way in which Scottish politics were tending to polarise as English politics had done and one remained with the interest with which one had embarked. This was part of the general tendency for Scottish politics to mirror what went on at Westminster. The Scots had been brought into union partly by English politicians who wanted to use them. The Scots in turn had wanted to use the English. In fact, by 1714, the outcome was that the Scots looked very much as if they were becoming prisoners of the English party structure.

The growing whig and tory division in Scotland was fairly short-lived largely as a consequence of its breakdown in England. That the incipient party development in Scotland collapsed so much more dramatically was due in part to its more recent appearance, partly to the antagonism between Argyll and the squadrone and even more to the Fifteen. In

England toryism became splintered and discredited but not by any means annihilated; in Scotland many supporters of the former ministry had shown themselves as active jacobites and went for a time into eclipse. When they or their sons emerged things had changed. As a consequence of the whig schism in England and the rule of Walpole, Scotland had, like England, reverted to a new version of court-country politics which was to last until the later part of the eighteenth century. As a result, in local politics, a man could call himself what he liked but what counted at Westminster was whether he was for the administration or against it. The new court-country structure in Scotland was built upon the Argyll-squadrone feud which had ante-dated the whig division in England, arising as it had done before the union. The animosity between these two groups, due in the main to Argyll's determination to assert himself and to dominate Scotland, would have led to trouble anyway but the quarrel amongst the whigs in England provided them with an excuse for a public brawl instead of hidden malice. Swift to take advantage of this rebirth of the old system were the detached natural insiders who had never relished the concept of party loyalty in or out: Seafield who wanted no part in struggles between Argyll and the squadrone, the Dalrymples who were never anything but a Dalrymple party and anyone else, like many of the nobility at the Hanoverian succession, who wanted to be free to apply for a job if he needed one. Men of this stamp could merge into court-country politics whereas in strictly party politics they were out of place.

What happened to the magnates after the Union is clear up to a point. The Union had one of its designed effects and in the long run as a threat to political stability they were finished. Their capacity for disruption, so menacing in the smaller kingdom with an independent parliament, was destroyed. Some reasons for their decline are straightforward. Their strength in British politics was in direct proportion to their electoral influence measured by United Kingdom standards and the votes they influenced at Westminster. Clearly they could not hope to cause the sort of

upheaval in British politics as they had done in those of
Scotland. The reduction of Scottish representation from
something over two hundred in all to sixteen peers and
forty-five commoners limited the number of members any
Scottish peer could hope to dominate. Even control of a
burgh no longer meant returning a member since the burghs
were divided into districts. So the large electoral interests
which were such a feature of the old parliament, such as
Queensberry's own personal following, estimated at over
thirty in 1704, were no longer possible. Apart from this the
process of political and administrative assimilation consequent upon the union meant that some of the contrivances
whereby magnates had influenced Scottish politics were
either abolished, as were the Treasury and the Privy Council,
or capable in time of being influenced from the centre like
the Court of Session, the new Court of Exchequer or revenue
patronage.

Not everything was due to the Union, of course; as
always in politics some part was played by biological
accident. However large an interest it was not of much use
unless in the hands of someone with the will and ability to
use it. If not carefully tended an interest went into a decline.
Queensberry died in 1711 leaving a minor as heir; Hamilton
was removed in a duel the following year also leaving a
minority. The Atholl family's equivocal role in the Fifteen
damaged its standing. Montrose's influence was reduced by
the disinclination of the first duke to live in Scotland. At a
lower level the Annandale interest was eclipsed in due course
by the illness of the second marquis and the insanity of the
third. Absenteeism, English education and marriage alliances
with English families took further toll producing an
anglicised nobility with ambitions not greatly different from
those of English peers.

All this is apparent; more interesting are the reasons
why some magnates continued to function so long after the
Union. Why did Queensberry, for instance, retain his
influence after the Union? And what about the house of
Argyll?

There are signs that Scottish magnates still hoped to

play a great part in the politics of the United Kingdom after 1707. Few peers were content with the possibility of election as one of the sixteen. Queensberry and Argyll took care to secure their own elevations to the English peerage before the union. There was such a queue hoping for this sort of promotion it is probable that promises had been made which would in part account for the serious nature of the Hamilton peerage crisis. Queensberry fought savagely for the post of Third Secretary until he was appointed, finally, in 1709 largely because he could cause more trouble than Montrose, the other contender. He then conducted another campaign to claim more than mere Scottish duties for the third secretaryship and to share in the profits of the two other secretaries. He won because Godolphin had made him an essential part of his system of management thereby exciting the jealousy of other nobles. Hamilton joined Harley in 1710 as an attack on Queensberry's position, Queensberry having been his rival long enough. Likewise Argyll's involvement with Harley was really a challenge not only to Queensberry but also to Marlborough which indicates the extent of his ambition. It was almost like the old days.

This recognition of some magnate power in the early years of the Union stemmed from two aspects of Scottish government pulling in opposite directions. It was necessary to reduce the magnate interests, which is what the Union had been designed, at one level, to do. Ideally the solution would have been to ignore the magnates after the Union and concentrate management in the hands of a central and homogeneous court interest on which everyone who needed favours would have been dependent. This was a solution continually urged by one court adviser or another. But under Godolphin this was not possible. He, Marlborough and, until his dismissal, an increasingly dissatisfied Harley, were attempting to defend a beleaguered court interest, preserving its freedom of action against junto attacks. Scotland had, at the same time, to be kept under control especially since, with the party balance as it was at Westminster immediately after the Union, the election of sixteen peers and forty-five commoners could not be left to chance. As there was no possibility of creating an undivided and powerful managing interest at the centre Godolphin had to fall back on what instruments were to hand; he virtually farmed Scotland out to the old court party ruled by Queensberry in return for its support at Westminster. All the weight and ingenuity of which the court was capable was placed behind Queensberry who could not manage Scotland alone. As Dartmouth later said, Godolphin managed Scotland like a colony, farming out its government to a subordinate interest responsible to the English court[15] but not, let it be said, too closely supervised. In this fashion Queensberry till 1710 preserved some status as Third Secretary whilst Hamilton and Atholl had difficulty in keeping afloat and Argyll devoted his time to military matters, quarrelling with Marlborough and plotting to undermine Queensberrry as he had tried to do before in 1705 and failed.

The first attempt to run Scotland entirely from Westminster was made by Oxford. Even whilst Queensberry was nominally Third Secretary he by-passed him after 1710 and attempted to centralise in the Treasury all Scottish administration and patronage. To help he used unofficial agents, but mainly John Scrope, an Englishman and a baron of the Scottish Exchequer, without formal responsibility. Had it been feasible to manage Scottish revenue and elections from the Treasury by the will of the Lord Treasurer alone Oxford would have achieved a triumph of management. It was not possible. He had too much else to do which meant neglect and neglect bred discontent. Nor had the Scots lost the habit of looking for some intermediate channel of patronage for which a near-anonymous baron of the exchequer was no substitute. The danger was that if Oxford failed to establish a grip on Scottish management someone else would. Yet, when this threat drove him to make changes in Scotland he carefully avoided working through magnates. Atholl was made Privy Seal but given little voice. Argyll and his brother, although former allies, were limited and then excluded which, as always, put them in opposition. The real task of management was given to Seafield as Chancellor and Mar as Secretary. Both were courtiers and servants who, as

Oxford knew from personal experience, were of proved competence in management. They were, also, dependent on him and not powers in their own right.

On the accession of George I a not dissimilar policy was followed. Seafield and Mar went, naturally. Yet a Secretary was expected and one was appointed: but not Argyll or his brother, Islay, determined leaders of a strong interest. Montrose was given the job, a duke with territorial influence but not of the stuff of which magnates, or even for that matter politicians, were made. As soon as he came under the inevitable attack from Argyll he resigned in a huff and withdrew to the office of Keeper of the Great Seal and, almost, from politics altogether. After an interval he was replaced by Roxburgh, a minor figure compared with Argyll and the representative of the squadrone, despised by many in Scotland and perhaps deservedly so; it produced far more than its fair share of incompetents, dilettantes and the merely idle. The aim of the United Kingdom administration seems to have been to have somebody in the secretary's office comparatively easy to control.

It was during this period and the accompanying subterranean warfare between Argyll and the squadrone that it became apparent how much of a nuisance a magnate interest could still make of itself if it tried, especially if it could count on some allies at the centre. The Campbell brothers fought to extend and then to preserve their interest in Scotland by every means open to them. At the 1715 election they were involved in a scheme to play for jacobite support by unofficially sponsoring an address for the dissolution of the Union. Argyll did his best to turn the Fifteen into an instrument for his own advancement. He took the opportunity to demand the lord lieutenancy of Dumbartonshire which Montrose regarded as his right as Argyll knew he would. This was the issue over which Montrose resigned. As commander of the government forces against Mar, Argyll accused the squadrone, perhaps with reason, of keeping him short of troops. However, at the same time he was declining all offers of assistance from squadrone interests on the spot apparently with a view to claiming that he had received none. He tried to obtain discretionary powers to pardon jacobites who surrendered so that he could acquire goodwill from both sides. Later, he espoused the cause of leniency to rebels in opposition to Roxburgh who, to keep favour in London, had to preach severity.[16]

After the rebellion he flaunted his independence rather too much and incurred the wrath of the king as a result of his friendship with, and supposed influence over, the prince. When, as a consequence, he and his brother were dismissed in 1716 they were able to demonstrate how effective the ramifications of an entrenched interest could be as an obstacle to the central government. They were helped by the fact that the Scottish political world still expected one interest to be in charge of patronage. There was continual speculation about which interest it would be and bets were placed accordingly. Since it was becoming increasingly clear that the ministry could not manage without Walpole and that there was a possibility of a change at the centre many chose to put their money on Argyll and Islay. The Campbell brothers exploited to the full what amounted to a confidence trick by means of which they produced the maximum amount of administrative inertia in Scotland when it came to obstructing Roxburgh. In the face of it Roxburgh found himself completely impotent; he took refuge in ignoring the situation and abandoned himself to petty intrigue at court and the enjoyment of his place. Baillie of Jerviswood, his nominal ally, was disgusted. So even in opposition the Campbells seemed to be getting the better of the squadrone.

When the major opposition to Walpole's advancement had disappeared through death or disgrace, he was able to give consideration to Scotland. The distribution of Scottish posts had fluctuated according to the state of the power struggle in England. Walpole had not been well-disposed towards Argyll and his brother but he was even less so to the squadrone, particularly to Roxburgh who, as an ally of Carteret, intrigued vigorously against him. And Roxburgh was still Secretary of State. The malt tax riots of 1725 provided an opportunity for Roxburgh's dismissal. Once again no Third Secretary was interposed between the central government and Scotland. There remained the problem of Argyll — a sizable one which lay at the root of Walpole's dilemma over Scotland.

It was desirable to continue as far as possible the policy of control from the centre begun after the Union by Oxford, supported by Scrope — by now Walpole's chief advisor as secretary to the Treasury — and in 1725 welcomed by Duncan Forbes who rejoiced at the abolition of the third secretaryship. Yet there was also the disquieting fact that the Argyll interest would not be ignored. To some extent Walpole was the prisoner of Scottish expectations. There had to be a dominant interest, the Scots thought; since Roxburgh had just been dismissed it could hardly be the squadrone so it had, therefore, to be Argyll. The past taught and the future was to confirm that the Argyll interest was attacked or ignored only at the risk of unsettling Scotland politically, which was the last thing Walpole wanted. Walpole was himself in a position to know what had happened under Anne. Then there had been the trouble the Campbell brothers had created for the squadrone secretaries. There were to be the complications resulting from Argyll's change of sides over the period 1736—40 which reached a climax in the 1741 elections. With the Argyll interest split between the duke and his brother who remained on Walpole's side, the opposition took twenty-six out of the forty-five Scottish seats which contributed greatly to Walpole's fall.[17] There was to be the paralysis of Scottish government after Tweeddale's appointment as secretary in 1742 when, from 1742 to 1746, as between the residual Argyll influence and Tweeddale, a secretary of little natural authority and considerable incompetence, nobody knew how things stood. The effect of this in Scotland was disastrous, making the Forty-five more serious than it might have been if it did not actually cause it.[18]

The policy attempted by Walpole was probably intended as a transitional measure. Some management advice and execution was necessary in Scotland. The management, to suit Scottish opinion, had to be done by someone with prestige who was seen to have the confidence of the central government beyond the possibility of being stabbed in the back. As things were this had to involve the Campbells yet there could be no overt handing over of Scotland to the Argyll interest. What was done had to be seen to be done at the will of the central government then perhaps in time the Scots would learn to look to the centre. This was an operation which all central governments, if they hoped to maintain themselves, had to carry out at some time or another against local powers not content with restricted influence. The Duke of Argyll himself could hardly play the leading active part in this arrangement. He was cast too much in the mould of an old-style Scottish magnate — peremptory, a table-thumper with a military insistence on instant obedience. His later behaviour in opposing Walpole ostensibly for the sake of Scottish interests does not have to be put down to his having seen any form of nationalist light. It was clamorous self-assertion quite consistent with all his earlier behaviour. Nothing that he did in the 1730s and 1740s was unprecedented in his career. His blackmailing of Walpole in 1733, exacting a price for his abstention in the Lords rather than going into direct opposition, had many precedents. His abrupt resignation in 1742 was also completely in character. Argyll was not really the man to employ in the management of Scotland if one valued a quiet life.

Walpole's decision was to place some confidence in the duke's brother, Islay, but without giving him the office of secretary which he had expected. Over the period of his influence Islay functioned as Keeper, first of the Privy Seal and then of the Great Seal. It was made plain to him that the trust placed in him must be exercised under central control and he accepted on those terms.[19] On the surface this would seem to have been a reversion to the policy of ruling Scotland through a trusted servant — a Seafield or a Mar. There is this difference: Islay was the representative of a powerful interest and they were not. This raises questions. Was Walpole wise to make so close an alliance with the Argyll family? Islay might very well send obsequious letters to Walpole and Newcastle but how far could they really control him? How could he be prevented, whatever Walpole's intentions, from being the 'uncrowned king of Scotland' that legend represents him as having been? Only when the Scottish problem as it appeared to Walpole is fully appreciated can the wisdom or otherwise of his policy and its continuation by Pelham be evaluated. It is difficult to see what else Walpole could have done that would not have been worse. The Argyll interest was 'overmighty'. Probably Walpole would have preferred it merely to have gone away but it was there and had to be coped with. It is most unlikely, particularly with Scrope at his elbow, that he contemplated any return to Godolphin's system of farming out Scotland. There is some significance in his choosing Islay, the less authoritarian of the brothers and the one gifted with more political tolerance. Islay was able to come to terms with most people if they would meet him somewhere near half-way, which gave him something in common with Seafield. It was a rare quality in his family.

As to the amount of power Islay wielded, officially or otherwise, there is no easy answer. He acquired a certain notoriety in managing the elections of the Scottish peers but this was a rather exceptional task. The list of peers to be elected was always a court list and Islay was merely an agent. In commons' elections inevitably, as the representative of the Argyll interest, holding office and with access to both Walpole and Newcastle, he and his agents were powerful enough. It was a good interest to be well in with and therefore exerted a natural pull. And it would be expecting too much of human nature to assume that Islay did not extend his personal interest in Scotland despite instructions emanating from Westminster if he thought he could get away with it.[20] But none of this was in essentials different from the way in which an English duke ran his interest. Some of his power was due to his relations with the government, some to his own territorial influence and jurisdiction, especially on the death of his brother when he succeeded as third Duke of Argyll, and some to his family connections, that with the Earl of Bute, for example, which extended his electoral interest. As in England, though, a regulating device was the multiplicity of electoral interests, each with access to the centre, cultivating its own territory, jealously guarding its sphere of influence and warning off all others as the Grants warned off Duff of Braco from Elginshire in 1741, telling him to stick to Banffshire which was his and they would deal with Elginshire which was theirs.[21] Such men were exceedingly jealous of their own prestige. They wanted for themselves, directly and not through intermediaries, any merit to be acquired by returning men from their territories who would support the court; this applied particularly where the dispensation of patronage was concerned. Sometimes, if his local position were threatened such a court supporter might need assistance. It was possible that he could get it from Islay either on his own judgement and initiative or as instructed from the centre. It was not unlike the way in which English court peers could fall back on treasury influence when their own did not suffice. But the Earls of Sutherland and Seafield supported the court anyway, directly, and needed no intermediaries. Selkirkshire was the stomping ground of men who were courtiers in their own right: Murray of Philiphaugh and Pringle of Haining.[22] There were the Queensberry and Annandale interests in Dumfriesshire and that district of burghs. None of these men was dependent on Islay; they happened to be in the same boat and rowing the same way.[23]

There were other practical limitations on his power. In some places the court had little electoral influence of its own: Berwickshire all the time and Dumfriesshire when the Annandale interest collapsed and Queensberry went into opposition in 1734. Again, local electoral management was sometimes only loosely connected with central government in that behaviour at Westminster was only one of the considerations involved in an election. Various interests, including the Argyll interest, had sometimes to settle for supporting whoever was likely to win an election rather than lose face by unsuccessful opposition. In Haddington burghs and in the county, Islay's lieutenant, Lord Milton, had to come to terms with the Dalrymple interest even when it was on the other side. Inverness-shire could not be controlled without Lord Lovat's sanction. Even after his execution on a charge of complicity in the Forty-five and with the Master of Lovat in prison for the same reason, the Master had to be visited in Edinburgh castle and asked rather bizarrely to support the government candidate without being given a promise of clemency.[24]

From 1747 there is considerable evidence of the third Duke of Argyll's obliging attitude to Henry Pelham who looked upon him as a most complaisant grandee: '. . . You will be surprised', he wrote to Newcastle, 'how little the duke of Argyll insists upon for his own people and how compliant he is with all those this ministry can depend upon, be they friends of his grace or his enemies . . . ,[25] Pelham seemed to be turning with relief to the Walpolian accommodation after a period of stress produced through tinkering with Scottish arrangements. Nevertheless Argyll — as Islay has now to be called — could drive a hard bargain. Overruled by the court when he wanted Areskine made President of Session, he was able to trade his acquiescence for the disposal of other posts. It took a deal of persuasion and sizable compensation to gain his assent to the abolition of the heritable jurisdictions in 1747. Complaisant, but still a power to be reckoned with as Newcastle discovered on Pelham's death when he began to make changes to the detriment of success in managing the Scots in 1755–6.[26] The third Duke of Argyll was the last of the overmighty subjects in Scotland. His family interest could not be ignored and therefore it had to be put to use, but under such restraint as could be exerted from the centre and by other interests. Any other solution would have produced trouble, so Walpole had little choice. Such opposition as developed in Scotland, especially after 1734 was not a direct result of Walpole's Scottish management; it was merely the pattern at Westminster exerting influence on the Scots. Marchmont, Montrose and Stair were not in opposition in despair at their deprivation of influence but because they had become allied to the English opposition and were playing the old country game, turning to account the 1734 election, Porteous, or whatever else cropped up. Apart from his rents Montrose's concern with Scotland was fairly limited anyway at this time.

And if it is true, as it may be, that Argyll spoke with two voices, one in Scotland and one in England, to get his

27

own way, it seems to indicate that Walpole's policy was likely to work sooner or later. Even the Duke of Argyll, like Walpole, had to take the situation as he found it, but if the only way to exert influence was to pose as the court's humble servant the most likely result in the long run would be for reality to correspond to the pretence and the house of Argyll would be no more troublesome than most English ducal families.

People who outlast the conditions in which they were raised and flourished are always an embarrassment and Argyll was no exception. Walpole in 1725 was right to hope that if the Campbell brothers did not collapse then at least in time they would fade away. A whole line of English ministers and administrators would have agreed with him. The power of Archibald, the third duke, did fade but neither Walpole nor anyone else can be blamed for not foreseeing that he would live till 1761. Then it could be said that the various pressures exerted by the Union, social and economic as well as political, had extinguished the old style Scottish magnate, and that the problem to which William had addressed himself after the revolution had disappeared.

NOTES

1. O.R.F. Davies, 'The wealth and influence of John Holles, Duke of Newcastle, 1694–1711', *Renaissance and Modern Studies,* ix (1965), pp. 22–46.

2. *Hist. MSS Comm. [HMC],* 46, *Johnstone,* p. 96, Johnston to Annandale, 22 March 1694.

3. *A Selection from the Papers of the Earls of Marchmont in the possession of the Right Honourable Sir George Henry Rose* (London 1831), iii, 103, Polwarth to Lord J. Murray, 14 May 1696; Nottingham University Library, Portland Collection, PwA 682, the same to Portland, 16 May 1696; *State Papers and Letters addressed to William Carstares,* ed. J. McCormick (Edinburgh 1774), pp. 219–21, Sir J. Ogilvy to Carstares, 24 July 1697; Buccleuch Muniments at Drumlanrig, Letters to the Duke of Queensberry, xiv, Lord J. Murray to Queensberry, 7 May 1696; ibid., Ogilvy to the same, 22 May 1696. I am indebted to the Duke of Buccleuch and Queensberry for permission to consult and make reference to these papers.

4. British Museum, Additional MSS, 6420, f. 17.

5. Cromartie in *Two Letters Concerning the Present Union From A Peer in Scotland To A Peer in England* (1706) described and denounced such tactics with which he was well-acquainted having in his time employed them all.

6. *The State of Scotland Under the Past and Present Administration With Relation to England & C.* (1703).

7. *HMC*, 72, *Laing*, ii, pp. 95—6, [c. 1704].

8. *Lord Belhaven's Speech, 2 November 1706.*

9. G.S. Holmes, *British Politics in the Age of Anne* (London 1967), pp. 391—4.

10 *HMC*, 71 II, *Finch*, ii, pp. 292—3, [July or August 1690].

11. By now officially Earl of Findlater and Seafield but it seems easier to refer to him by the title under which he is best known.

12. As Harley had become in 1711.

13. *HMC*, 60 I, *Mar and Kellie*, i, p. 505, Mar to the justice clerk, 7 August 1714; ibid., pp. 509—10, the same to lord Grange, 20 November 1714; National Library of Scotland [NLS], MS. 5072, 24, [Mar] to Sir J. Erskine, 7 September 1714.

14. Scottish Record Office [SRO], Clerk of Penicuik Muniments, GD 18 3153, 16 April 1715.

15. G. Burnet, *History of His Own Time* (Oxford 1833), v, p. 362, Dartmouth's note.

16. Much of this can be followed in the letters to Montrose from Rothes during the 1715 election campaign (SRO, GD220) and from Mungo Graham of Gorthie during the rising (ibid.). See also Wood's letters to Bennett over the same period (SRC, GD 205).

17. J.B. Owen, *The Rise of the Pelhams* (London 1957), p. 7 n.2.

18. Rosalind Mitchison, 'The Government and the Highlands, 1707—1745' in *Scotland in the Age of Improvement*, ed. N.T. Phillipson and Rosalind Mitchison (Edinburgh 1970), pp. 37 et seq.

19. Public Record Office, SP54/16, 344, Islay to Newcastle, 11 November 1725, for example.

20. John M. Simpson, 'Who Steered the Gravy Train, 1707—1766?' in N.T. Phillipson and Rosalind Mitchison, ed., op. cit., pp. 47—69, argues that he did get away with it most of the time.

21. *The House of Commons 1715—1754*, ed. Romney Sedgwick (HMSO 1970), i, p. 385.

22. Ibid., p. 393.

23. The argument that these were effective checks would seem to receive support from J.R.M. Sunter in 'Stirlingshire Politics, 1707—1832', an as yet unpublished Ph. D. thesis (Edinburgh 1972).

24. *The House of Commons 1715—1754*, i, pp. 386, 400.

25. Quoted ibid., p. 160.

26. Simpson, art. cit., pp. 61—2.

Administration and Law

ATHOL L MURRAY MA LLB PhD

Assistant Keeper, Scottish Record Office

The subject of administration and law is so closely related to Dr Riley's that it could be regarded simply as another aspect of the same thing. Statesmen work through the administration to achieve political ends and the administration can be used as a means of gaining or maintaining political power through patronage or otherwise. Laws are made or repealed by politicians in Parliament and both before and after the Union it was possible for the law to be used for political ends. These factors form a constant background to the subject matter of this paper, though it will not always be possible to deal with political influences in detail. Dr Riley has elsewhere shown the working of these influences in the years immediately following the Union;[1] this paper will look at the impact of Union in the longer term, for it has played a large part in shaping the country in which we live today.

Our guide for part of the way will be Sir John Clerk of Penicuik, who died in 1755 at the age of 79, after a lifetime of close involvement in public affairs, both before and after the Union. Landowner, mine-owner, antiquary, patron of art, poetry, music and architecture, there were few fields in which he did not take an acute and well-informed interest. Here, however, we are mainly concerned with him as a lawyer and administrator, the two roles being closely blended in the office of Baron of the Exchequer in Scotland which he held for well over forty years.[2] He was an attractive personality, with an engaging brand of commonsense, illustrated by a marginal note in his private memoirs: 'I hate egotisms if I do not avoide them, but as this account of my own life is not to be published I must use them or throw away my pen'.[3] His son was dispatched to boarding school with much sound advice, including 'to avoid swiming and to remember that more good swimers are drowned than those who know nothing about it'.[4] The school was Eton, for which Sir John had good practical reasons. 'I comforted my self in doing what I thought wou'd prove most for his improvement and advantage, for besides a fine opportunity of learning the Greek and Latine, I thought it wou'd be an additional qualification to him that he understood the English language, which since the Union wou'd always be necessary for a Scotsman in whatever station of life he might be in, but especially in any publick character.'[5] For Sir John had himself been one of the Scottish commissioners for negotiating the Union, and he was a fervent supporter of it. In this he was not self-seeking, but rather he believed that closer links with England would confer great benefits upon his native land. Whether or not Belhaven and Fletcher of Saltoun make a greater appeal to patriotic instincts, it is at least arguable that in the circumstances of 1707 Clerk had a better understanding of what was practicable.

Clerk believed that Scottish independence was already lost before 1707. 'As to our civil government, it was an entire state of dependence on the Councils of England. We had frequent sessions of Parliament, a constant Privie Councill, a Treasury and Exchequer, but all these subservient to such administratiors as the chief ministers in England thought fit to recommend to the Soveraign'.[6] Certainly since the 1688 revolution policy was often decided by the sovereign and his or her advisers in the light of the interests of England and her continental allies. So too under Anne the crown's own freedom of action was increasingly limited by the need to maintain a sizable backing for the ministry in the English parliament. The administration in Scotland took its orders in the form of royal letters and warrants countersigned by the Secretary of State, who acted as its link with the sovereign and ministry in London.

But the administration in Edinburgh played an essential part in the work of government both in providing information and in undertaking the day-to-day running of the country. It is only necessary to mention two branches of it in particular, namely the Privy Council and the Treasury. The Privy Council had a large membership, between forty and fifty, so that one might say it was more of a disgrace to be left off it than an honour to be put on. But a large part of this membership was indeed honorific, for in 1691 there was difficulty in even getting a quorum of nine for some meetings.[7] Anyone who has read through its records will be conscious of the sheer triviality and tedium of a great proportion of its business, evidence indeed that the really important issues were being decided elsewhere.[8] On the other hand it had the judicial powers which the English council had lost with the suppression of the Star Chamber. As Clerk says 'The Privy Council...was sometimes arbitrary in their proceedings yet was such as contributed very much to keep up the face of government and preserve the peace of the country'.[9] The Treaty (article 19) retained it 'for preserving of public peace and order, until the Parliament of Great Britain shall think fit to alter it or establish any other effectual method for that end.' In the event parliament took only a few months to think fit to abolish it, which took effect a year to the day after the Union. Its abolition was a by-product of party manoeuvering at Westminster and was hastened by the influence which it would have brought to bear on the forthcoming elections.[10] It was, however, hasty and ill-considered, for it proved impossible to establish any other 'effectual method'. Two experiments, the Commission of Chamberlainry and Trade and the Commission of Police, were wrecked because basically no politician wished to see created a body which might allow someone else to control Scottish patronage and influence Scottish elections. The Commission of Police did indeed survive until the later part of the eighteenth century. Apart from lending its name and prestige to some projects for public works, it did little except provide its members with a dignified title (Lord of Police) and excessive salaries. In 1727, however, its more important economic functions were hived off to the Board of Manufactures which had a long, successful and useful life in which it became the parent or step-parent of such diverse bodies as the Fisheries Board and the National Galleries of

Scotland.[11]

There is no doubt that the disappearance of the Privy
Council was regretted. Years later Clerk wrote of the
complaint 'that by takeing away the Privy Council of
Scotland there is very little of Government to be seen
amongst us. This complaint I am affray'd is too well founded,
for tho' the peace of the country be in the hands of certain
justices of the peace as in England, yet there are some shires
in this country where they doe not meet at all, and there are
others where I am affray'd they meet to oppress one another
either as justices of the peace or as commissioners of
supply'.[12] The abolition of the Privy Council was one —
though only one — of the factors leading to the
disappearance of the office of Secretary of State for
Scotland, but here again control of patronage was probably
crucial. The old line of communication between London and
Scotland was thus severed at both ends. Eventually a new one
emerged in the Lord Advocate, who, as the link between the
ministry and the Scottish legal administration, extended his
control to patronage and other matters. Formal responsibility
for Scottish administration, other than financial, was vested
in the Home Office from 1782 until the creation of the
Scottish Office a century later.

Financial business in pre-Union Scotland was the
responsibility of the Treasury. Like its English counterpart it
had evolved rapidly since the 1660s and was beginning to
exhibit the characteristics of a modern government
department. It had taken over the more important
administrative functions of the Exchequer, though the latter
was still of importance as a court of law for matters affecting
the revenue. Apart from a few years in the 1680s the office
of Lord High Treasurer remained permanently in commission
and, says Clerk, 'The Treasury was under the direction of
those who had the chief authority in their hands and were
often men of that capacity that it was a pity they had noe
more to manadge than what the revenue of Scotland
produced'.[13] Just how much the revenue did produce is a
mystery, as the Treasury accounts after 1692 were never
finalised or audited. Even at the best of times there was an

imbalance between revenue and expenditure, the former being calculated in 1682 as £91,477 sterling per annum, and the latter as £93,718.[14] This got worse as Scotland had to foot the bill for the Glorious Revolution and King William's foreign wars at a time of economic depression. Various expedients such as hearth tax and poll tax produced little effect upon the growing burden of debt. On the most favourable estimate Scottish revenue at the Union amounted to some £110,000 sterling, with a prospective increase to £160,000 in consequence of it. But these figures are suspect as they were calculated with a view to determining the Equivalent, the compensation due to Scotland for taking on a share of England's National Debt and bearing increased taxation.[15] Yet if we set even £110,000 against the £66,000 required for the pay of the army alone under its 1702 establishment of approximately 3000 officers and men,[16] apart from the cost of clothing and equipment, and add on the civil establishment and other charges of government, we must reach the conclusion that in 1707 an independent Scotland was not financially viable. One must not forget too that England bore the cost of the royal household, diplomatic representation overseas and the pay of Scottish regiments serving outside Scotland.

The first and most important effect of the Union was that it stopped this financial mess getting worse and eventually helped to put it right. Not only was money sent up in 1707 to pay the forces.[17] Not only were the accumulated debts eventually paid off out of the Equivalent, though after considerable muddle and delays.[18] The true impact of Union was that it cured the basic fault of Scotland's finances. This was, that lack of money made for a weak and ineffective administration, and that a weak and ineffective administration was in no position to raise more money. The price of reform, as indeed of Scotland's admission to the English trading area, was acceptance of the English revenue system. This was in itself no bad thing, for the English customs and excise services had well-developed techniques and professional expertise. Though nominally-independent Scottish Boards were set up in 1707 they were for long dependent on their English counterparts for trained personnel, general guidance and advice. In fact they were merged in single Boards for the whole United Kingdom between 1723 and 1742. They were also subject to overall Treasury control, more particularly in the case of the customs, where patronage even of minor posts was vested in the Treasury.[19] The first Scottish commissioners exhorted their officers: 'For the cheerful and punctual performance of your duty in the present employment wherewith you are entrusted, you have an essential encouragement from the reasonable hopes of such further advancement as you shall be found capable of upon representation of your behaviour to the Lord High Treasurer of Great Britain, who is a lover of Method, and an encourager of virtue.'[20] Though method and virtue alike were often found wanting, the new customs adminstration did lay a foundation for future improvement. Notably, in spite of some quite monumental frauds by merchants and collectors, it successfully introduced a heavier and more complex system of duties and trade control and it extended this control to areas such as Orkney and Shetland and the north west Highlands and Islands which had had to be virtually written off before the Union.

Treasury control of Scottish revenue and expenditure is one impact of the Union which has lasted with little diminution until the present day. There was no place in the new system for the old Scottish Treasury, which continued on an interim basis for one year only. It then gave way to an Exchequer which was re-modelled by statute to be a simplified copy of the Westminster Exchequer. 'Simplified' is only comparative, for some of its features only make sense, if at all, when viewed against the historical background of the English Exchequer. Why bother with a Pipe Office, which had little to do except give an accountant a formal discharge? Why did the Auditor of Exchequer not audit some accounts, such as Excise, which had its own auditor, and sheriffs' accounts, which were audited by the Lord Treasurer's Remembrancer? There were some major points of difference from England. For instance there was no Lower Exchequer, so that incoming revenue was held by the Receiver-General of

Land Rents, the Receiver-General of Customs and the Cashier of Excise until they were authorised to pay it out again.[21] Also the Exchequer retained certain specifically Scottish functions, defined by the Treaty (article 19) as the 'power of passing signatures, gifts, tutories, and in other things as the Court of Exchequer at present in Scotland has'.[22] Lastly the Barons of Exchequer, who formed the new court, had certain administrative or ministerial functions, which put them in the position of a sub-treasury. Within fairly tight limits set by the United Kingdom Treasury they supervised the various collectors of revenue and the Scottish revenue boards, issued warrants for payments, managed the crown lands and exercised some minor patronage in disposing of university bursaries and charitable payments. They also reported on matters referred to them by the Treasury.

Though the new Exchequer dealt with routine matters quite efficiently, it did not make any great showing otherwise. Partly this could be blamed on the English element among the Barons and other personnel, who were often absent from their posts for long periods. They could usually find pressing official, political or personal reasons for not coming to Scotland. Baron Scrope was so useful in London that he was eventually appointed Secretary of the Treasury.[23] In March 1739 we find William Bowles, the King's Remembrancer, who should doubtless have been in Edinburgh himself, writing from England to tell Clerk that Lord Chief Baron Lant, who suffered from gout, 'designs in a few days to retire to Chiswick for 5 or six weeks to drink asses milk in order to prepare him for his northern journey'.[24] Some of the blame at least lies with the Treasury for the extent to which they restricted the Barons' freedom of action, though to be honest we still can see today one awful warning of what the Barons could do when they were allowed. They decided that a stone slab roof would be cheaper than lead for the chapel royal at Holyroodhouse; unfortunately the fabric of the building could not stand the additional weight and the chapel stands a roofless ruin to the present day.[25] But the Treasury kept control over the civil establishment and would only allow the Barons to grant warrants for payments which they had authorised. They were, however, extremely dilatory in granting such authority in special cases. So we have the truly sad case of James Smith, who had been surveyor of public works since 1692. After the Union he found that his salary could not be paid because it had been accidently omitted from the civil establishment. Accordingly he went to London in 1710 and petitioned Godolphin, who referred the matter to the Scottish Barons, who in turn put in a favourable report. Soon afterwards, however, Godolphin fell from power, and Smith had to start all over again with Oxford. Oxford agreed that he should be paid for 1708 and 1709 but thought that subsequent payments should be deferred until the new civil establishment was ready 'which by reason of the Queen's death (which happened soon after) was never done'. Why Smith did not make an effort to be put on George I's new civil establishment is not explained but he continued to carry out his duties conscientiously even though he was not being paid, until 1719 when, at the age of 73, he went off to try his luck at the Treasury once more. He got to London only to find that he was no longer surveyor and his post had been given to someone else. Still he lodged his petition, hoping at least for his arrears of salary 'which hath been hitherto deferred from time to time these eleven years last past to the great discouragement of your petitioner and his numerous family of thirty two children'. The Barons, to whom the matter was again referred, lost little time in submitting a favourable report and, though Smith was not re-instated, the Treasury did at least pay him his back money.[26]

Perhaps the Treasury regarded Scottish business as something of a nuisance, which could be put to one side as long as possible. As Scrope wrote to Clerk on 20 December 1715, 'Nobody here understands anything of our affairs and I can find nobody that hath leisure enough to receive information'.[27]

The Barons were given more discretion in the management of the Forfeited Estates after the '45, where they were conspicuously more successful than the commissioners who had been appointed after the '15. Clerk was aware of the problems in dealing with these estates, such as the attachment of the inhabitants 'to the family for the forfeiting person which they regard as their Sovereign, their God and their All'.[28] But the Barons were limited to managing the estates pending their ultimate disposal by sale or by annexation to the crown. The larger estates, like Lovat, Cromartie and Perth were annexed to the crown and put under special commissioners, who had wide powers to manage them for the benefit of the inhabitants and the nation as a whole. Agriculture was improved, fishing and industry encouraged, roads and bridges constructed, schools and medical services provided. The estates were eventually handed back to the representatives of their former owners, the administration being wound up by the Barons, who supervised the expenditure of its surplus funds on public works.[29]

The reconstruction of the Scottish Exchequer also involved its judicial functions which were brought into line with the Exchequer court of England. Article 17 of the Treaty had expressly provided that 'the laws concerning regulation of trade, customs, and such excises, to which Scotland is by virtue of this Treaty to be liable, be the same in Scotland, from and after the Union as in England'. It was therefore logical that two courts administering the same body of laws should have similar composition and forms of proceeding. There was, however, this difference: the jurisdiction of the Scottish court was confined to revenue matters and it did not, like its English counterpart adapt its procedure to attract business from other courts. For the rest assimilation to English practice was carried through with what one could describe as an inspired dottiness. As long ago as 1599 the Scots had decided that the logical date for beginning the New Year was New Years Day, 1st January. In 1708 the clock was literally put back and the Scottish Exchequer adopted the English practice of beginning the year on 25th March. The court proceedings were mainly written in Latin, a language which the Scottish civil courts had abandoned by the mid-fifteenth century. Some of the records were engrossed on parchment rolls, which the Scottish

Exchequer had finally discarded in 1672 and they were written in court hand, that highly-specialised, contorted script which makes English judicial records undecipherable to the layman. If it seems incredible that a medieval survival of this sort should have been introduced deliberately as late as 1708, it is even more incredible that anyone looking at the records has to contend with not one variety of court hands but three, as the various Exchequer offices produced their own specialised brands. Latin and court hands were both swept away in 1733 as part of a similar reform in England. The writs and forms of pleading and procedure remained unchanged, apart from translation from Latin. In fact some of them survived the demise of the Court of Exchequer and its final amalgamation with the Court of Session in 1856. English habits of thought survived transplantation to a Scottish setting. As late as 1810 information laid against Highland crofters for having illicit stills described the offender as, say, 'Donald Munro of Fearn in the county of Ross, *Yeoman*'.

Though the re-modelled Exchequer had its ludicrous aspects, one cannot fault the basic assumption that a court administering revenue statutes, which were largely framed with reference to England, should be governed by English law and precedents. Few of the cases it dealt with, seizures of smuggled goods, informations for infringement of revenue statutes, recovery of debts due to the crown, appear to have presented much legal difficulty and in the majority the facts were so clear that no defence was attempted. The Barons were, however, involved with Scots law in their ministerial or non-judicial capacity, in respect of grants of land charters, leases of crown lands and gifts of property falling to the crown by escheat or as last heir. Lawsuits relating to such grants nevertheless fell within the jurisdiction of the court of session. Because of its dual responsibilities the court always had a mixed Scottish and English personnel. Clerk says 'We assisted one another with our advice, and what knowledge of the laws we had attained in either nation, so that every thing was transacted amongst us with great friendship and unanimity, as well as justice'.[30] Clerk's grasp of the law became such that he was co-author, with his English colleague Scrope, of the standard work on the Scottish Exchequer.[31] Though eminently well qualified he failed to achieve his ambition of becoming Lord Chief Baron. The first Lord Chief Baron in 1708 had in fact been a Scotsman, Seafield, who, says Clerk, 'having always daubled in politicks, tho' often in an awkward way, was so far imposed on by the Ministry of Great Britain at that time as to be persuaded to lay down his commission in order to qualify himself the better to be chosen one of the sixteen peers of Scotland. This plot against him was that the prime minister and his friends might appoint one of their own nation to succeed him'. But Clerk found the Englishman, Smith 'vastly superior to the Earl in learning, wisdom and discretion, so that we who were his brethren in the Exchequer lived very happily with him'.[32] In 1728 the post went to Matthew Lant 'by the interest of his friends in England', says Clerk, who describes him as 'a poor, harmless, timorous man'.[33] At the next vacancy in 1741 Clerk had high hopes, as he had the active support of Argyll and Walpole among others. Once more he was disappointed, for the post went to another Englishman, John Idle, who had the support of the Lord Chancellor. We may sympathise with Clerk's own sad comment: 'those who have friends in any great offices in England will always be preferred to any Scotsman'.[34] It was small wonder, however, that a correspondent reported that Idle 'seems perplexed and embarrassed about coming down to Scotland'.[35] Not until 1775 was the post once more given to a Scotsman, Sir James Montgomery of Stanhope, but his successors were all Scots. One judge of the court, known appropriately as the English Baron, had to be a member of the English bar. For more than a century the successive English Barons received a handsome allowance on top of their salary, presumably to compensate them for the hardship of exile in Scotland. At last in 1819 the Commissioners on the Courts of Justice in Scotland thought it their duty 'to express the opinion which we entertain that the provisions made in respect to an English baron are no longer essential or requisite.[36]

We have dealt at length with the court of Exchequer

because it was the one part of the judiciary which was open to English influence. The courts of Session, Justiciary and Admiralty were expressly continued by article 19 of the Treaty and in the case of the first two at least judicial appointments were only open to members of the Scottish bar. The same article contained the oft-quoted provisions that 'no causes in Scotland be cognoscible by the Courts of Chancery, Queens-bench, Common-Pleas or any other court in Westminster Hall'. Needless to say this was tried. On 5 March 1708 an English writ was issued for the purpose of removing a case of adjudication of prize, which had been tried by the Admiralty Court in Scotland and which had been confirmed by decree of the Court of Session, to be re-examined before a quorum of councillors appointed by the Queen. But the Court of Session considered that the writ 'had been obtained and passed as a matter of course, by surprise, and that there was no necessity to take any public notice thereof; but at the same time, that their silence might not in any wise be interpreted to be prejudicial to the right and authority of the Court of Session established for the administration of justice and good of the subjects within Scotland, they did unanimously declare, that they nor their clerks were not held to give obedience to the said writ, and that they held themselves in duty bound, by their trust, to maintain and preserve the privileges of the Court of Session or College of Justice, to which they were sworn at their admission'.[37]

Article 19 also preserved the jurisdiction of the inferior courts. The only change to be noted is the revival and strengthening of the justice of the peace courts (originally borrowed from England by James VI) as a necessary instrument for enforcing revenue statutes, particularly those relating to excise. No special provision for them was made in the Treaty but an act of 1707 (6 Anne c. 6) 'For rendering the Union of the two kingdoms more entire and complete' laid down that the justices 'over and above the several powers and authorities vested in the justices of the peace by the law of Scotland, shall be further authorized to do, use and exercise, over all persons within their several bounds, whatever doth appertain to the office and trust of a justice of peace by virtue of the laws and acts of parliament made in England before the Union, in relation to, or for the preservation of, the public peace: Provided nevertheless, that in the sessions of the peace the methods of trial and judgements shall be according to the laws and customs of Scotland'. However the J.P. courts were, and have remained, of little consequence in Scotland, probably because their jurisdiction has overlapped with the burgh and sheriff courts.

The sheriff courts were greatly improved in consequence of the Act of 1747 (20 Geo. III c. 43) abolishing heritable jurisdictions, that is judicial offices or jurisdictions held as private property. This act was in clear breach of article 20 of the Treaty, which provided that 'all heritable offices, superiorities, heritable jurisdictions, offices for life, and jurisdictions for life, be reserved to the owners thereof, as rights of property, in the same manner as they are now enjoyed by the laws of Scotland'. The '45 provided a pretext for abolition. Some of the major jurisdictions, stewartries and regalities, had already fallen into the hands of the crown; others were enjoyed by Hanoverian supporters, such as Argyll. The baron courts, some of which had exercised powers of life and death within living memory, were preserved with greatly limited competence. Holders of baronies still had the right to recover rent from tenants in their own courts, but the courts themselves gradually ceased to function in the second half of the eighteenth century. In 1822 the Commissioners recommended that the Barons' powers 'of deciding themselves, or by bailies whom they appoint, in questions where they themselves have a direct patrimonial interest, and which therefore is still competent by the existing law, should not be left to fall into desuetude, merely by the silent operation of more enlarged and equitable views, but that a power so inconsistent with the general spirit of the Jurisdiction Act, although the situation of the country might possibly render it necessary when the Act was passed, should in future be withdrawn and abrogated, by express enactment to that effect'.[38]

One can count the 1747 Act as an effect of the Union.

No doubt an independent Scotland would have had to face the same problem before the end of the century but it is doubtful whether the opposition of the jurisdiction holders could have been overruled or bought off so effectively. One major effect of the Act was the reform of the sheriff courts, not merely by the removal of the heritable sheriffs but also by the extinction of the competing jurisdictions of stewartries, regalities and bailiaries within the territorial areas of the sheriffdoms. This, and the vesting of the appointment of the sheriffs, still called illogically sheriffs depute, in the crown, enabled a firm foundation to be laid for the modern sheriff court system. This was a reform conceived in purely Scottish terms — there was not and still is not, any comparable English system.

From law courts we must now turn to substantive law. Here the Union had little initial impact, nor indeed was it intended to, for article 18 of the Treaty had laid down 'that the laws which concern public right, policy and civil government may be made the same throughout the whole United Kingdom; but that no alteration be made in laws which concern private right, except for evident utility of the subjects within Scotland'. So apart from necessary tidying up to bring revenue laws into line with England there was little legislative interference with Scots law, except the notorious restoration of church patronage in 1712. There was indeed little point of contact between the legal system of the two countries. Originally very similar, Scots and English law had developed in a widely divergent fashion since the thirteenth century. Where the English barons had closed the door to outside influence with the words *'nolumus leges Anglie mutare'*, Scotland had received and assimilated considerable tracts of Roman and canon law. Where the English courts were still tied to the rigid medieval forms of action, the late development of the Court of Session had given Scotland a central civil court which had more flexible procedures and which could administer both law and equity. Where English law had become inbred and inward-looking, Scots lawyers had looked for training to the law schools of the continent and for ideas to the great European jurists. The traffic was

43

not one-way either; Craig on feudal tenure and Welwood on maritime law were names which were known and respected on the continent as well as in their native country.[39]

With all this, however, Scots law in the early seventeenth century had been something of a rag-bag of ideas from various sources. But the first of the great institutional writers, notably Stair, by judicious selection, innovation, and borrowing from other systems had transformed it into an integrated and consistent body of doctrine. This work was continued during the eighteenth century until, in the nineteenth, the ending of the former close contact with the continent and the growing English influence on legislation and judicial decisions set Scots law upon a different course. Scottish criminal law too, though expounded by the 'Bloody Mackenzie', was by far a more logical and humane system than that of England, a characteristic which it maintained until the present century.[40]

To put the matter in simple terms, in the last forty years before the Union Scots law had developed into a system which was peculiarly well adapted to resist English influence, even without the formal safeguards in the Treaty, while English law had little to commend it in a country to which it had not been carried, as it had been overseas, by conquest or colonisation. Except for actual legislative interference, such as the Treason Act of 1709 (7 Anne c. 20), which substituted a barbarous code for one perhaps equally barbarous, English penetration was only possible in the limited fields where Scots law was as yet undeveloped or defective, such as patent or copyright law. Patent law provides an interesting example. Separate Scottish patents were necessary until 1852 but very few were granted prior to 1760 and the majority of those after that date simply extended to Scotland an existing patent which applied only to England. Though they were issued from the Scottish chancery in Edinburgh, the warrants on which they proceeded were prepared by the Home Office in London and their terms and conditions were almost identical with English patents.[41] The first major English importation, however, came in the field of mercantile law in the early nineteenth century. Though both Scottish and

English Law could be regarded as particular branches of a universal Law Merchant, George Joseph Bell, who was the first great authority on the subject in Scotland, relied to a great extent on the judgements of Lord Chief Justice Mansfield and his successors in the English courts. Nevertheless it is fair to point out that Mansfield, a Scotsman by birth though not by education or legal training, had drawn upon Stair and foreign jurists for general statements of the principles of jurisprudence which he could not find in existing English authorities. For this, he was, in fact, attacked both then and later by those who upheld the native virtues of English law.[42] Bell was himself aware of 'some danger lest the purity of mercantile jurisprudence, and the integrity of our own system of law, should be impaired by too indiscriminate a use of English authorities'. But he did pride himself 'that I have introduced or facilitated a knowledge of the English cases to students of the law of Scotland, and contributed to that most desirable object, in the present state and relation of the two countries, — a gradual, and, at last, a perfect assimilation of the English and Scottish jurisprudence'.[43] However, given the innate sense of superiority of English lawyers of his day, such assimilation was bound to be one-sided and through the influence of Bell and others like him the impact of Union on Scots law in the nineteenth century was towards the adoption of English principles.

Assimilation also came through the agency of the House of Lords as the supreme appelate tribunal from the civil courts of both England and Scotland. It is notorious, however, that the Treaty of Union was silent on the whole subject of appeals. This omission was almost certainly deliberate and Sir John Clerk, who was involved in the negotiations, makes the rather ingenuous comment: 'It was thought sufficient by the Articles of Union to guard against bringing our civil actions before any of the judicatures in Westminster Hall'. He admits that the number of Scottish appeals could be regarded as a grievance, 'but such, indeed, is the justice of the high judicature I have named that there is noe body in this country who would not desire to have all

their actiones both civil and criminal determined there'.[44]
The House of Lords, however, drew the line at criminal
appeals, though one was attempted as late as 1876. Like
Clerk, Sir Walter Scott believed in the merits of the right of
appeal to the Lords which 'has, no doubt, had its influence in
forming the impartial and independent character which, much
contrary to the practice of their predecessors, the Judges of
the Court of Session have since displayed'.[45]

We should, however, stop to consider the nature of the
tribunal which both Clerk and Scott commended. It was not,
as it is today, composed of specially appointed, experienced
judges drawn from all parts of the United Kingdom, but, in
theory, of the whole body of peers. Scott's *Bride of
Lammermoor* turns upon a Scottish appeal just after the
Union, and he makes his hero say 'It is in the House of
British Peers, whose honour must be equal to their rank — it
is in the court of last resort that we must parley together.
The belted lords of Britain, her ancient peers, must decide'.[46]
Now it is true that there were cases where the 'belted lords'
did decide, Greenshield's case in 1710 and Magistrates of
Elgin v. Ministers of Elgin, the only successful criminal
appeal, in 1713. In both these the House decided on party
lines, and the High Church Tories upheld episcopal clergy in
their defiance of the law, no doubt to teach both Scottish
presbyterians and English non-conformists a lesson. Scott
conveniently forgot this when he wrote that 'The high and
unbiassed character of English judicial proceedings was then
but little known in Scotland; and the extension of them to
that country was one of the most valuable advantages it
gained by the Union'.[47] But for the most part the general
body of peers was not interested in appeal cases, unless there
were special reasons for becoming involved, as in the
celebrated Douglas cause. Scottish appeals were left to the
Lord Chancellor and other lawyer peers. They might call for
assistance from English judges but no judge with Scottish
legal training sat in the House of Lords until the
mid-nineteenth century. Even the counsel for the parties
were English, until Scottish advocates started to make their
appearance in the later eighteenth century.[48] Given the

differences between Scottish and English law the arrangement
was not a happy one, particularly perhaps in those fields
where there was a superficial resemblance between the two
systems. For the English judges and counsel, however learned
in the Common Law, lacked detailed knowledge of Scots
Law and the other civilian systems with which it was linked.
In 1806 Lord Chancellor Erskine, who was a Scotsman by
birth, had to confess to the House of Lords 'I know
something of the law but of Scotch law I am as ignorant as a
native of Mexico; and yet I am quite as learned in it as any of
your lordships'.[49] At best such ignorance meant that English
judges had to translate a Scottish case into English terms so
that they could understand what it was about. At worst it
meant that English law was applied regardless. Some of the
worst examples of this occurred during the nineteenth
century. For instance the case of Bartonshill Coal Company
v. Reid in 1858 resulted in the English doctrine of common
employment being foisted upon Scotland, because, in the
words of Lord Chancellor Cranworth, 'if such be the law of
England on what ground can it be argued not to be the law of
Scotland? The law as established in England is founded on
principles of universal application not on any peculiarities of
English jurisprudence and unless therefore there has been a
settled course of decision in Scotland to the contrary I think
it would be most inexpedient to sanction a different rule to
the north of the Tweed from that which prevails to the
south.'[50]

The impact of English law through the House of Lords
was not lessened by the introduction of a Scottish Judge,
Lord Colonsay in 1867, and the reform of that tribunal by
the Appelate Jurisdiction Act of 1876 (39 & 40 Vict. c. 59).
In fact the Scottish Law Lords tended to embrace English
law with too great enthusiasm. Legislation, too, had its
effect, and the Sale of Goods Act of 1893 brought about that
assimilation to which Bell had looked forward, at the cost of
throwing a whole tract of Scots law into confusion by the
indiscriminate adoption of English principles. Further inroads
have been made in the present century as practitioners and
even some professors of Scots Law have fallen into the habit

of citing English decisions as authoritative in Scotland. The late Lord Normand warned that Scotland must not neglect the tradition of Roman Law, 'For unless our law continues to grow in accordance with that tradition it will run a grave risk of becoming a debased imitation of the Law of England, stumbling and halting before every new problem where we have no English precedent to guide us'.[51]

Yet over the last century and more the impact of Union has increasingly worked both ways and Scots law has provided judges and legislators with solutions for problems of English law. Lord Campbell's act, the Fatal Accidents Act of 1846, gave a right of action to near relatives, which already existed in Scotland. Divorce for desertion and legitimation by subsequent marriage of the parents both had a long history in Scotland before they were introduced into England. We might add the doctrine of diminished responsibility and majority verdicts in criminal cases from a long and increasing list of such innovations. English lawyers are now far more prepared to learn from another system. A last-generation Lord of Appeal, Lord Maugham, could still speak slightingly of 'those interesting relics of barbarism tempered by a few importations from Rome, known to the world as Scots law'.[52] This generation however, is typified by Lord Denning who speaks appreciatively of the lessons learned and still to be learned from Scotland.[53] For the next generation some writers have seen a new and important role for Scots law as a link between English law and the civil law-based system of the other common market countries. They may be over-optimistic, but it is significant that the government nominated a Scottish judge, Lord Mackenzie Stuart, as Britain's first representative on the Court of Justice of the European Communities at Luxembourg. Perhaps we have entered a new phase in the impact of Union on Scots Law.

In the century following the Union English judges were not uniformly hostile to Scots law and some indeed made an effort to understand it. There was, however, dissatisfaction with the Court of Session, whose structure and procedure was even more alien to English ideas and indeed quite far removed from those of the modern court. We tend to think of the number of appeals as a specifically Scottish grievance, though here the fault, if any, was that of Scottish litigants, from Lord Rosebery in 1708 onwards, who could not forgo this last chance of winning a lawsuit. But the House of Lords was also somewhat aggrieved that it should have to deal with higher relative proportion of Scottish cases than English appeals and tended to blame the Court of Session.[54] Even Lord Thurlow, who had considerable understanding of and respect for Scots Law told Boswell that 'there was no system of judicial forms more excellent than that of the court of Session in theory, or more detestable in practice'.[55] Earlier in the century Sir John Clerk had proposed, unsuccessfully, that the Court of Exchequer should be interposed as an appeal court between the Court of Session and the House of Lords.[56] The momentum for change gradually increased. In 1788 we find Boswell reflecting on the lack of a 'grateful return from my country for my animated interposition to preserve the Court of Session'.[57]

One of the main objects of reform was the introduction of civil jury trial into Scotland. This would automatically cut the number of appeals, because there could be no appeal against a jury's finding of fact. One would like to know how Clerk would have viewed this innovation. Used as he was to working with juries in the Exchequer Court, he appears to have had no high opinion of their infallibility.

'Let us but reflect a little what mischiefs ignorant, bad, or unwary Juries have brought upon the trade of this part of Britain since the Union of the Kingdoms in 1707. They have on many occasions found wine to be Spanish that not only the taste and flavour, but by the concurring testimonies of many witnesses, has been found French come from Bourdeaux. They have found the best kind of French brandies to be Dutch spirits. They have found ships to be forced by stress of weather into our ports, when the contrary appeared by witnesses, charter-parties, invoices, coquets, letters, instructions, and other plain documents. They have found foreign soap, starch, &c, to have been sold in a fair way of trade, when it appeared they were sold in by-places, and sometimes in the night after a very clandestine manner. Thus

Juries by fraudulent or mistaken notions of trade, and tenderness to smugglers, have ruined a vast many families, and brought a real loss on the trading people of this country to the extent of £300,000; whereas, if they had set out as they ought after the Union with honour and conscience, and with a just regard to the laws, they might have crushed in the bud this pernicious trade of smuggling, and consequently done the greatest service imaginable to the trade and manufacturers of their own country'.[58]

It was, however, possible for the court to order a new trial where the verdict appeared to be contrary to the evidence. Despite the rather unfavourable experience in the Exchequer there was a persistent feeling in some quarters in Scotland that jury trial in civil causes was one of the good things which ought to be imported from south of the Border.[59] Lord Chancellor Eldon wrote scornfully in 1807 'Let me observe that I have read up the Scotch modern publications eulogising the trial by jury. Not one of the authors know what it is, and they . . . have totally forgot that the Court of Session is a court of equity as well as law'.[60] Modern writers have blamed Eldon for foisting civil jury trial upon Scotland[61] but his letter to the Lord Advocate shows that he saw its actual and potential drawbacks in England as well as Scotland: 'I must excuse myself — I do not know that some enthusiasts in this country would excuse me — if I say that I can see nothing in some instances in which we have trial by jury, but grievous delay, enormous expense and gross injustice'.[62]

His letter was prompted by a bill reforming the Court of Session, which he had read 'with amazement again and again as the worst and most ignorantly and imperfectly drawn legislative composition that I have seen'.[63] His objections to it were so manifold that he wrote a second letter on the following day. The bill proposed dividing the court of session into three divisions headed by an extraordinary Lord of Session and setting up a new court of review above it.

'The more I think of it the more I doubt whether there can be a division of the court of session without some tampering with the Articles of Union. But the system at present proposed for a court of review looks so like a job that it will be certainly deemed a job, and it is really an affront to the president [of the court of session], which is painful to think of, and I cannot satisfy myself that making a president over him who, by the constitution of the court, is the president of the whole court, is not somewhat more than tampering with the Articles of Union. . . . With all its faults and imperfections, however, unless there is great exertion on the part of Scotland, this bill will be carried. The exclusion from consultation of all who ought to have been consulted both here and in Scotland proves a design which cannot be misunderstood'. He concludes, 'I am sorry for you gentlemen north of the Tweed but I fear we are going to bestow kindnesses upon you which you had better be without'.[64]

Despite Eldon's fears, the bill did not pass in its original form. In 1808, however, the Court of Session was reformed by splitting the Inner House into two divisions, and various other changes between that date and 1825 produced broadly the system which exists at the present day. Civil jury trial was eventually introduced in 1815, but a separate semi-independent tribunal, the Jury Court, was set up headed by the English-trained Lord Chief Commissioner Adam. It was not a particularly successful innovation but by one of those paradoxes which seem to mark the impact of Union, jury trial still survives in Scotland for types of cases in which it has been abolished in England.[65]

The creation of the Jury Court saw the Scottish judicial establishment at its greatest extent. There were fifteen Court of Session judges, some of whom received supplementary salaries for acting as commissioners of the jury court and lords of justiciary. The justiciary court was nominally presided over by the Lord Justice General, the Duke of Montrose, who was handsomely paid in this sinecure. There were five Barons of Exchequer, one of whom was also Lord Chief Commissioner, a Judge Admiral presiding over the Admiralty Court who could act by deputy, and four commissaries of Edinburgh who had exclusive jurisdiction in consistorial matters such as divorce cases. This gives a total of twenty-six persons, holding an even larger number of high judicial offices. In modern terms there was clearly a great deal of over-manning and hidden redundancy. This was no new thing. In Clerk's day the Exchequer court 'had only 4 terms or sessions in the year, and few of them exceeded 3 weeks, so that nothing cou'd be better calculated for my humure than the office I enjoyed'.[66] But this attitude could not be maintained in the nineteenth-century atmosphere of retrenchment and reform. It may well be, as Lord Cockburn alleged, that the Court of Session acquiesced in the destruction of the other courts, in clear breach of the articles of Union, to preserve their own positions and salaries.[67] Certainly by 1840 the Lords of Session, reduced from fifteen to thirteen and doubling up as Lords of Justiciary, were the sole survivors. First to go was the Admiralty Court in 1830, its prize jurisdiction having been taken from it already, by decisions of the House of Lords and administrative actions of the Treasury. In the same year the Jury Court was merged with the Court of Session. The commissary court was finally suppressed in 1836 by which time it had lost the greater part of its judicial powers. When a Baron of Exchequer died or resigned he was replaced by a Lord of Session as Exchequer judge, though the Court of Exchequer was not formally abolished until 1856. With the death of the Duke of Montrose on 30th December 1836 the office of Justice General was permanently merged with that of Lord President of the Court of Session.

Retrenchment occurred elsewhere in the civil establishment. The Edinburgh Mint was effectively closed by an Act of 1817, having been maintained for over a century at a cost of £1200 per annum, without producing a single coin since 1710. By a curious piece of lip-service to the Treaty of Union the Act directed that as the various posts fell vacant the duties of the Scottish officers should be taken over by the corresponding officers in the London Mint without extra salaries. In this manner the fiction of a Scottish Mint was preserved until as recently as 1971.[68] The Mint was not the only victim of administrative reform. The separate Scottish Boards of Customs and Excise were suppressed in 1823 and replaced by United Kingdom Boards. The Barons of Exchequer lost their administrative functions to the Treasury and the Commissioners of Woods and Forests, and the various Offices or departments within the Exchequer were abolished or merged until by 1848 only two remained. One of these, that of Presenter of Signatures, disappeared in 1874, the other, the Queen's and Lord Treasurer's Remembrancer's Office still remains to the present day, having acquired in the interim other responsibilities, such as the *Edinburgh Gazette* and the registers of limited companies and business names. It is another of these paradoxes that the Scottish Exchequer survives, as a modern government department with a history going back over 700 years, while the English Exchequer, on which it was remodelled in 1708 and from which the very title of Queen's and Lord Treasurer's Remembrancer was derived, has long since vanished. While we may count the administrative centralisation of the early and mid-nineteenth century as a belated impact of Union — for it was surely implicit that the centre of administration must be at the centre of political power — that centralisation was never complete. Because of Scotland's special problems and perhaps more so because of its separate legal system some administrative functions always remained in Edinburgh. So Scotland retained a Fisheries Board, a Prison Board and other agencies, which were to form the basis of the Scottish Office and of administrative devolution after 1886.[69]

Nevertheless with the creation of a new Scottish adminstration some remnants of the old remained at risk because they were, or could be represented to be, unnecessary. These included household offices which could have had little if any purpose since James VI left Scotland in 1603 — the royal physicians and apothecary and the Under Falconer, the last by a royal warrant of 1840 which alleged that its suppression 'would afford relief to our loyal subjects in the islands of Orkney and Zetland';[70] offices of state — such as Lord Clerk Register and 'Lord Privy Seal; offices which were still of some use even in the nineteenth century, such as the Master of Work, but which did not fit in with a modernised administration. This process continued well into the present century with the Re-organisation of Offices Act of 1928[7][1] which suppressed the Deputy Clerk Register and Director of Chancery, though the Scottish Chancery, the origins of which go back to the twelfth century, still exists within the Department of Registers of Scotland.

The impact of Union was greater on administration than on law because Scotland in 1707 had a well-developed legal system but a rudimentary and weak administration. Perhaps a cleaner sweep could have been made at the Union but the old offices which were preserved and some of the new ones which were created afforded scope for political patronage and provided for another century a refined form of national assistance for the nobility and landed gentry of Scotland. Hence the nineteenth century reforms swept away much which was useless and indefensible.

Perhaps the summing up is best left to Lord Cockburn, whom we may see torn between Scottish patriotism and Whig reforming zeal. He is writing in 1832.

'The Exchequer has died, like our other useless Courts, lamented by those who think that the glory of the kingdom is impaired by the abolition of ancient institutions; keenly defended by the friends of patronage; sighed over by the expectants who look to the law solely for those judicial sleeping places; and thought by reasonable men to have lived at least long enough. There are many who lament the disappearance of institutions which reminded us of our old royalty, and attested to our old national independence. I sympathise deeply with this feeling; insomuch that if there could be any security that the offices we have lost would have been distributed as rewards to deserving men, I would have been for keeping all of them. Against that nothing could be said except that they were useless and cost a little money. A few comfortable sinecures, when not created, but coming by descent and in connection with historical recollections, make a poor country respectable. Our king, and our parliament, and our nobility have left us, and the capital has a poor church, no trade and an unendowed college. Our Commissioners of Excise, and Commissioners of Customs, and Judge-Admiral, and Consistorial Judges, and Exchequer with its countless claws, and Admiral on the North Station, and Justice-Generals, and Lord Registers, not as now mere names, were gentleman-like things. They must, many of them, have fallen no doubt under the scythe of economy sooner or later, but they would not have fallen as they have done, unwept by the disinterested, had it not been for the use to which they had been long turned; but corruption for the sake of faction was their sole object and their sole effect. They were a mere price in the hands of Government to seduce electors, and the seduction was practised with such atrocious openness and such disgusting success that our lingering reverence for the fragments of our ancient state was lost amidst our indignation at the baseness of which it was productive'.[72]

NOTES

1. P.W.J. Riley, *The English Ministers and Scotland 1707–1727* (London 1964).
2. J.M. Gray ed., *Memoirs of the Life of Sir John Clerk of Penicuik*, Scottish History Society [SHS] (Edinburgh 1892), *[Clerk's Memoirs]*.
3. Ibid., p. 52.
4. W.A.J. Prevost, 'A Scotch boy at Eton in the early eighteenth century', *Etoniana* no 124 (1971).
5. *Clerk's Memoirs*, p. 87.
6. 'Sir John Clerk's observations on the present circumstances of Scotland 1730', ed. T.C. Smout, *Miscellany*, x, in (Edinburgh 1965), p. 184, *[Clerk's Observations]*.
7. *Register of the Privy Council of Scotland* (3rd series), xvi, p. 600.
8. See, for instance, the summaries of council business in the introductions to *Register of the Privy Council*, xiv–xv.
9. *Clerk's Observations*, p. 184.
10. Riley, *English Ministers*, pp. 94–6.
11. Ibid., pp. 177–87.
12. *Clerk's Observations*, p. 203.
13. Ibid., p. 184. See also A.L. Murray, 'The Scottish Treasury 1667–1708', in *Scottish Historical Review*, xlv (1966), 89–104.
14. Ibid., p. 104*n*.
15. *Acts of the Parliaments of Scotland*, xi, app. 196.
16. SRO, Treasury Register, E.7/9, p. 117.

17. *Calendar of Treasury Books*, xxi, part ii, pp. 343, 445.
18. Riley, *English Ministers*, pp. 203—29.
19. Ibid., pp. 123-39.
20. *Instructions for the collectors and other officers employ'd in Her Majesties Customs etc. in the north-part of Great-Britain* (Edinburgh 1707), p.32.
21. J.E.D. Binney, *British Public Finance and Administration 1774—92* (Oxford 1958), pp. 233—7.
22. Riley, *English Ministers*, pp. 75—86.
23. *Dictionary of National Biography.*
24. Clerk of Penicuik Muniments, GD18/2863/27.
25. J. Harrison, *History of the Monastery of the Holy-Rood and of the Palace of Holyrood House* (Edinburgh 1919), pp. 238—40.
26. SRO, Treasury Reports, E.307/2, pp. 126—31.
27. SRO, Clerk of Penicuik Muniments, GD18/2857/6.
28. *Clerk's Memoirs*, 259.
29. V. Wills ed., *Reports on the Annexed Estates* (HMSO 1973), pp. v—xv.
30. *Clerk's Memoirs*, p. 259.
31. *Historical View of the Forms and Powers of the Court of Exchequer in Scotland*, by Baron Sir John Clerk and Mr Baron Scrope (Edinburgh 1820). Clerk's original MS is in SRO, Clerk of Penicuik Muniments, GD18/2850.
32. *Clerk's Memoirs*, p. 73.
33. Ibid., p. 166.
34. Ibid., p. 166.
35. SRO Clerk of Penicuik Muniments, GD18/2863/41.
36. *Sixth Report of the Commissioners on the Courts of Justice in Scotland* (House of Commons, 1819), p. 11.
37. *Fourth Report of Commissioners . . .* (1818), p. 36.
38. *Eleventh Report of Commissioners . . .* (1822), pp. 5—6.
39. *Sources and Literature of Scots Law*, Stair Society (Edinburgh 1936), pp. 61—63, 330—1.
40. Ibid., pp. 63—6, 372.
41. G.J. Bell, *Commentaries on the Law of Scotland* (1858 edn), pp. 536—46.
42. Lord Denning, *Borrowing from England* (David Murray Lecture, Glasgow 1963), 5—19; but see T.B. Smith, *British Justice, the Scottish Contribution* (London 1961), pp. 47—9.
43. Bell, *Commentaries* (1821 edn), pp. xvi, xviii.
44. *Clerk's Observations*, p. 210.
45. *Bride of Lammermoor*, ch. xvi, note.
46. Ibid., ch. xvi.
47. Ibid., ch. xv.
48. A.D. Gibb, *Law from over the Border* (Edinburgh 1950), pp. 8, 15—16.
49. Ibid., p. 49.

50. Ibid., pp. 58—9.
51. T.B. Smith, 'Strange Gods', in *Juridical Review*, iv (1959) p. 141.
52. T.B. Smith, *British Justice, the Scottish contribution* (London 1961), pp. 47, 142, 150, 215.
53. e.g.*Borrowing from Scotland.*
54. Gibb, *Law from over the Border*, pp. 46—7.
55. *The Private Papers of James Boswell* ed. G. Scott and F.A. Pottle (Yale edition), xviii (1934), p. 245.
56. *Clerk's Observations*, p. 211.
57. *Private Papers of James Boswell*, xvii (1933), p. 90.
58. *Forms and Powers of Court of Exchequer*, pp. 272—3; cf. *Clerk's Observations*, p. 211.
59. I.D. Willock, *Origins and Development of the Jury in Scotland*, Stair Society (Edinburgh 1966), pp. 247—51.
60. HMC, 72, *Laing MSS*, ii. p. 703.
61. Smith, *British Justice*, p. 73; Willock, *Jury in Scotland*, pp. 255—6. Eldon's views in 1807 were doubtless coloured by his antipathy to a Whig measure and he did support the eventual introduction of jury trial in 1815.
62. *Laing MSS*, ii, p. 703.
63. Ibid., p. 709.
64. Ibid., p. 710.
65. Willock, *Jury in Scotland*, pp. 252—62.
66. *Clerk's Memoirs*, p. 73.
67. H. Cockburn, *Memorials of his time* (Edinburgh 1909), pp. 206—9.
68. 57 Geo. II c.67. By the Coinage Act of 1870 the office of Governor of the Mint of Scotland was vested in the Chancellor of the Exchequer until this Act was repealed by the Coinage Act of 1971.
69. Sir David Milne, *The Scottish Office* (London 1957).
70. SRO, Register of Privy Seal, PS.3/15 p. 283.
71. 18 & 19 Geo. V. c.34.
72. *Journal of Henry Cockburn* (Edinburgh 1874), p. 35.

The Union and Economic Growth

R H CAMPBELL MA PhD

Professor of Economic History, University of Stirling

Past generations dealt with the relationship between the Union and economic growth with fewer qualifications than their descendants do today. Sometimes they asserted that the Scots were starved into Union or, by way of contrast, that the Union was an act of economic statesmanship. Even today the Union may be regarded, in company with the organisers of this Conference, as 'the most vital event in the history of modern Scotland'. So it may be in political, cultural and administrative life, but in economic affairs it should be considered merely as a preparation for events which began only a generation or more later, and which reached their greatest historical significance in the last decades of the eighteenth century. On that interpretation, economic factors played some, though not necessarily the most important, part in the making of the Union, and its economic impact was no more than a final recognition of the mutual advantage to be found in the Scottish and English economies growing together, in alliance instead of in outright competition. The seventy-five years after the Union were not an economic desert but historians may have overemphasised the significance of a few economic events, particularly the earliest and quite untypical industrial developments. A catalogue of economic happenings will not produce a general explanation of the pattern of economic growth, especially when so many of the economic developments of the time, though small and insignificant by later standards, were hampered by an inadequate supply of capital.

The 'dearth of monies' which had been the cry of many Scots for centuries, remained a common characteristic of many enterprises in the eighteenth century, even though capital requirements were slight, especially when compared with later standards which the railways introduced. Agricultural improvements were not always profitable to the improvers, partly because any benefits accrued only after an exeptionally long period. So Cockburn of Ormiston found to his cost, and he had to sell to the Earl of Hopetoun in 1748. And the poineering modern industrial concern in Scotland, Carron Company, founded in 1759, survived several major financial crises in the first twenty years of its life only by the skin of its teeth.

The contribution of Cockburn or Carron are recognised because they employed methods which were to prove successful later, and so they seem to herald the beginning of a new age. But frequently technical experiment, and even technical success, was not matched by economic success. Hence perpetual injections of credit were required, and any interruptions to the injections brought periods of expansion to an end in the stop-go fashion of modern times. The result, to quote David Hume on one such occasion, was to 'reduce people to more solid and less sanguine Projects, and at the same time introduce Frugality among the Merchants and Manufacturers':[1] in short to reduce the rate of economic growth.

Such clear-headed observers of the economic scene as Sir James Steuart and Adam Smith fully appreciated the problem. Steuart would have shed few tears had any reduction of credit merely restricted 'the propensity of the rich to consume', but he knew full well that its harmful effects would fall on 'the disposition of the poor to be industrious'.[2] Smith, in his exposition of Scottish banking, applauded the issue of paper money as a device which enabled a country, poor as was Scotland, to increase the supply of credit, and so provide circulating capital to engender further increases in employment and income; otherwise the few industries to prosper would be those, such as the cattle trade, which were able to exploit rising demand without internal improvement.[3]

In resolving such a deadlock Scotland's unique banking system played a vital role. Its contribution may be challenged by questioning whether the banks provided financial stability at the price of conservative lending policies. But the banks' ability to lend was not entirely under their own control. It was limited by the ever present danger of an adverse rate of exchange leading to a drain on the reserves. Hence the maintenance of economic growth after the Union required the removal of any restraints imposed by a weak balance of payments position. An assessment of the Union's contribution to their removal requires the compilation of balance of payments accounts for Scotland after the Union and to do so exactly is impossible. An analysis of the balance of payments on current account can be based only on statistical information derived from customs accounts, which are comprehensive only from 1755, but which, in any case, exclude the vitally important trade with England. Knowledge of capital movements both long and short term is fragmentary, but their significance, especially their speculative nature, cannot be underestimated. Contemporaries alleged that such movements were responsible for some of the worst balance of payments crises of the eighteenth century, with all their consequences in restricting credit and in retarding economic growth.

The Union may well have increased the magnitude and destabilising influence of capital movements. New calls for the export of capital appeared. Remittances were made to residents in England, sometimes to expatriate Scots, for the age of the absentee landlord was at hand. The Scottish nobility had to be assisted in London as they tried to ape the political activities of their wealthier counterparts. Again, when London offered a higher rate of interest, Scottish investors were ready to remit capital there. Most significant of all, for most directly related to the Union, increased taxation, and remittances of part of it to London, was a new burden on Scotland.

To evaluate the overall significance of any one of these examples of capital outflow is difficult. The records of the exchequer and excise, so ably put at our disposal through the work of Dr Murray,[4] enable us to discuss fully, as an example, the problem of transfer of taxation; it is a good choice for other reasons, for probably no event after the

Union engendered such vociferous opposition, and such riotous behaviour, as the malt tax. The total amount levied in taxation increased, partly reflecting the level of economic activity in a fiscal system which relied on customs and excise duties, but it is not easy to substantiate the view that a heavy burden of transfer was placed on Scotland, for the amount remitted to London was not great. Only the land tax produced a substantial remittance. Apart from what was absorbed by the costs of collection, almost all customs revenue raised went to meet various debentures and bounties. Excise revenue, apart from maintaining the courts and other civil functions, went on a series of economic projects in Scotland. Even the controversial malt tax itself produced only £20,000 a year for London, and from 1727 any surplus over that amount was transferred to the Board of Trustees for Fisheries and Manufactures to encourage economic development. In sum, in the fifty years or so after the Union about 15 to 20 per cent (but very rarely any more) of the revenue raised in Scotland annually left the country. In normal times that was an insignificant burden to transfer.[5]

Not surprisingly, most of the complaints of contemporaries were about such outward movements of capital, for that seemed to cause so much trouble, but the Union also encouraged a compensating flow in the reverse direction. Dr Murray has pointed out how the Scottish Exchequer was saved from virtual bankruptcy by the Union.[6] In addition some capital flowed into the banks, for the Union facilitated access to London's greater financial reserves, and so to accommodation in periods of financial crisis, a source which tempered the Scottish banks' pressure on their domestic customers. Perhaps, as some suggested, the banks might have used the method even more extensively to avoid the need to restrict credit when the balance of payments was under pressure, but, as modern experience has demonstrated, the procedure, irrespective of its extent, was particularly useful for a country with resources as limited as Scotland's then were. Private capital also flowed north for investment, but in this case the evidence of the extent is so fragmentary that it is only possible to hazard a guess that there was a net

movement of long-term capital to Scotland, for few of the
Scots who went to make their mark in England took much
with them. But though there might have been a net inflow of
private capital in normal times, it was still potentially a
destabilising influence. Much of the investment was only
short-term, and was quickly withdrawn during periods of
crisis, as in 1762, when it was alleged that about £500,000
had been invested by Englishmen in Scotland and that its
withdrawal to invest in government securities was a major
cause of the exchange crisis of that year.[7]

In sum then, capital movements probably increased with
the Union, but in both directions. At worst they may have
made difficult exchange situations more difficult. It is
unlikely they caused them. Their effect was marginal. Hence
the ultimate solution to the potential danger of an adverse
foreign balance lay in an improvement in the balance of
payments on current account, by some combination of
increasing exports and reducing imports.

The Union is often thought to have made its major
impact on economic growth in this field. Access to the
growing markets in England and her colonies provided
opportunities which were not available in the traditional
declining markets on the continent. Increased demand, such
as was provided by Scotland's inclusion within the privileges
of the Navigation Acts, provided a stimulus to indigenous
industrial development, and, though frequently a high degree
of initial dependence on the importing country may have
followed, the beneficial effects were not confined to a
narrow sector but were spread more widely. However, the
dangers of too facile reasoning about the effects of such
opportunities should be sufficiently well known to a
generation accustomed to the economic arguments for and
against entry to a common market.

Of the importance of foreign trade after the Union, at
least superficially, there is no doubt. That it was chiefly an
entrepot trade, with tobacco at its centre, is abundantly clear
when the full trade statistics first became available in 1755,
for then re-exports were 47 per cent of the value of total
exports. Thereafter they increased rapidly to 73 per cent of

the total in 1771, a peak year in foreign trade. The growth of the entrepot trade may be attributed to the Union, though only with some qualifications, but any consequential stimulus to economic growth in other sectors of the economy is less certain. The Glasgow merchants who traded with the colonies could not always find the goods they wanted to export in Scotland and had to call on supplies from London. Even Scotland's major export industry of linen, which contributed 20 per cent of the value of domestic exports in 1771, had to import linen yarn. More significantly, finished linen goods were imported, to be re-exported later. Imports from Holland and Germany were displaced, but not those from Ireland, which showed an upward trend in the second half of the eighteenth century.[8]

If the beneficial effect of the opening of markets by the Union is questioned in the case of the linen industry, then it is difficult to maintain there was a strong link between foreign trade and the rise of indigenous Scottish industry. The collapse of the re-export trade after 1776 confirms the sceptical interpretation. Trade with the West Indies replaced the trade with north America, but re-exports to the West Indies were much less important. Scottish products formed the basis of the trade, but they were such traditional goods as plain linen, haberdashery and fish. Though a more direct link was being forged between the country's foreign trade and its internal economic growth, the growth of foreign trade was not accompanied by any marked increase in the range of commodities. Hence there was duality in much of the economic activity of the eighteenth century. Many Scots opened the international markets which led to an extension of trade in the eighteenth century and later, and the Union helped them to do so, but their activities provided few unique advantages for Scottish economic growth. The opportunities were frequently for the economic growth of Scotsmen rather than for the economic growth of Scotland.

There are objections to such a negative interpretation. The dichotomy of the economy between external and internal development may not have been so extreme. In Glasgow, and other towns which benefited from foreign trade, a stimulus was given to a variety of small-scale new manufactures to supply goods merchants wanted to export, but it is important to stress that they did not represent the beginnings of the great staples of the later eighteenth century. And there were important indirect effects, for some of the profits earned in merchanting were invested in land and in some of the industrial ventures then frequently associated with landownership. That was hardly surprising in the eighteenth century, for industrial enterprises were still frequently based on the countryside and could easily be regarded as an aspect of landownership. A more significant objection is based on the undoubted benefits of trade with England, which the Union made possible, but which cannot be documented for lack of information. As the Alien Act showed before the Union, and as Adam Smith pointed out seventy years after it, trade with England in the two major exports of linen and cattle was vitally important, especially since the output of both could easily be increased without any significant internal changes or improvement. We do not know the quantities exported, but fragmentary statistics and qualitative evidence indicate that the opening of such markets proved to be the most immediate benefit of the Union and probably its greatest benefit in the long run. The rise of Scotland's foreign trade was certainly dramatic, but it is difficult to trace its contribution to the country's indigenous economic growth until the 1780s. There is no doubt about the importance of the connection with England. But, as Smith was fully aware, that stimulus to internal development was effective because the demand could be satisfied by even the low quality products of the Scottish economy of the time, and so, as well as being signal successes, the exports of linen and cattle to England also demonstrated the inadequacies of the Scottish economy.

Modern experience leads inevitably to concentration on the possibility of Scotland's balance of payments position on current account being strengthened by increasing exports. An alternative solution was to substitute home produced goods for imports, a remedy which might seem to be either a counsel of despair or a counsel of perfection. A counsel of despair, in so far as it was a reversal to policies followed and found wanting in the mercantilist conditions of the seventeenth century. A counsel of perfection, in so far as it required a removal of Sir James Steuart's dictum that 'those who are fond of foreign clothing will take the price of it from their bellies, to put it on their backs';[9] and the Union encouraged such tastes in many people.

One aspect of Scotland's ability to dispense with imports is, however, vitally important. When T.S. Ashton held that in England in the eighteenth century 'the coming of dearth was sufficient in itself to halt, or reverse, an upward movement of activity',[10] he was almost repeating Adam Smith's view that 'years of dearth ... are generally among the common people years of sickness and mortality, which cannot fail to diminish the produce of their industry'.[11] Hence the relevance of the changed agricultural conditions after the Union. Famine was never as general as it had been in the closing years of the seventeenth century; shortages occurred, but severe shortages were limited to particular areas, notably the Highlands. Prices of grain were stable until after mid-century and, as imports of grain declined, so exports increased. Such an optimistic interpretation of agriculture's ability to meet the new demands being placed on it cannot be maintained throughout the century; later, prices increased, and in some of these years of high prices substantial quantities of grain were imported into Scotland.[12] The provision of foodstuffs was not the only function of agriculture; it had also to provide some of the raw materials required for the country's earliest industrialisation. Domestic flax production was inadequate to meet the increased production of linen. In 1755 more than one-third of the value of retained imports was undressed flax.[13]

So Scottish agriculture, while able to avoid the famine conditions of earlier years, was in its unimproved state in much of the eighteenth century unable to support securely a rapidly growing urban population or produce adequate supplies of necessary raw material. Since agriculture was far and away the dominant sector of the economy, any resolution of the restraints of a weak exchange position, which was always a potential danger to economic growth, lay in agricultural change. The bottleneck of agriculture was the most critical of several which limited Scotland's ability to exploit opportunities opened by the Union. Through its elimination the way was opened towards self-sustained economic growth.

The historiographical problem of the early eighteenth century, and of the economic impact of Union is not one of producing yet more examples of economic growth, like rabbits out of a hat, for their total effect, especially on industrial development, was but slight. The historiographical problem is one of trying to determine how Scotland may have been prepared, particularly by the Union, to break through the restraints on growth. Such an explanation is essential, not only for an appraisal of the immediate impact of Union, but for an appreciation of the country's history until the later eighteenth century. Thereafter the economic growth of Scotland may be explained in terms similar to that of England, for by then the parts of Great Britain were so closely linked that any differences in their experiences were limited, unless the Scots were able, almost on the basis of personal qualities developed earlier, to exploit any openings available to them even more effectively: on the basis, in short, of the values and aspirations of society which helped determine the qualities of entrepreneurship.

Two aspects of Scottish life and thought — values and aspirations of Scottish society — helped determine the qualities of entrepreneurship. First, the remarkable contribution of what may be described, in the search for a term wider than technological achievement, as material creativity: the quality demonstrated in the eighteenth century and later by many Scots: the Adams, with their superb ability to design buildings of all kinds; Watt, with the steam engine and related devices; Rennie, Telford and the bridge-builders; the marine engineers; the shipbuilders. The technological contribution of the engineers, mechanical and civil, was directly relevant to industrial development, the steam engine being only the outstanding invention among several. The second aspect of Scottish society to be distinguished is the work of the social theorists, who tackled the problems of society and so produced the foundations of the modern social sciences.

The two elements of Scottish society can be related in a way which is seen to encourage the formation of effective entrepreneurial qualities. The intellectual and the industrialist, the scientist and the merchant, the banker and the lawyer, all lived in close physical proximity in a limited area of central Scotland, and the point, though elementary, cannot easily be over-estimated in an age of poor communications. Physical proximity encouraged intellectual contact, but that was of minor significance, for the two elements are intellectually complementary. At the most elementary level, the drive for rational social improvement led to the acceptance of change, economic or otherwise, among influential groups, whose resistance might have been critical. Attempts to transform the economy were only one aspect of much wider attempts to transform society. More positively, the acceptance of economic change in this way enabled the materialist creativity of the Scot to be fully recognised, expressed, and exploited. But, were these qualities the legacy of the Union?

Almost certainly the intangible concern with social reformation had nothing to do with the Union but was an indigenous quality, which may be associated with the Scot's interest in theology. It is possible to deplore that obsession for it might have had harmful economic effects by inhibiting any other activities by the Scots. If so, only its prior decline, and the acceptance of an ecclesiastical settlement at the end of the seventeenth century, released energies for economic enterprise. The connection may be neither so simple nor so negative. Preoccupation with propositional theology was preoccupation with the supreme social science for those for whom the acceptance of secularism had not compelled theology's displacement in pre-eminence by sociology or psychology. The propositions of theology are as concerned with social transformation as are those of sociology, especially when, in the protestant tradition, they begin with the personal transformation of the individual. Scottish theologians at the height of their influence, were certainly never averse to political or social theory, so the theological concern may be interpreted as an early aspect of social engineering, as one which is perpetuated and given new clothing by the increasingly secular values of the eighteenth century. To that extent the interest may be indigenous or long-standing. Whatever external links it had were, of course with the continent, whence came Dugald Stewart's 'constant influx of information and liberality'.[14] In that the theological tradition was allied to the other Scottish intellectual tradition of the law. Geneva and Utrecht were more important than English seats of learning in nurturing the distinctive qualities of the Scottish intellectual. Its origins are independent of the Union.

The other element fashioning the Scottish entrepreneur, the success in material creativity, is more difficult to explain but has to be understood within the framework of the theological obsession. It is easy to believe that the Scots' obsession led them to display little creative ability. The criticism is valid only if confined to an apparent lack of achievement in what, in the language of the two cultures, can be regarded as artistic activities, the imaginative arts. No such clear-cut distinction could be drawn in the eighteenth century, but the undoubted closure of a number of areas of cultural self-expression, for whatever reason, left the Scots to find cultural achievement in material creation. The repression of the imaginative arts among the Scots by the theologians may be regretted, but in compensation the repression encouraged the qualities requisite for economic success and provided an environment in which these qualities could operate successfully. There was economic gain to offset what some consider to have been cultural loss.

Indigenous or European as the qualities forming the entrepreneurs were, they were of a nature which the Union was bound to influence, for it confirmed, though it did not initiate, the increase of cultural, as well as economic, links with England and the New World instead of with the continent. Contact with the continent was not lost. But the evidence of the increasing cultural influence of England after 1707 is, of course, widespread. Education was completed in England instead of on the continent; the precepts of the common law began to infiltrate into Scotland. That is condemnation enough for many; it is the evidence of the Union's destructive influence on any native Scottish culture, perhaps killing finally any lingering life which remained after the alleged repression by the theologians. The compensation may well have been similar, by continuing to force the Scots to find cultural satisfaction in economic achievements. More positively the English influence may have inculcated a more tolerant streak into Scottish intellectualism, which, while it accepted, even welcomed, social change, could still accommodate that change to the existing social structure. It is remarkable that, for all the Scot's tendency to degenerate into being an argumentative, metaphysical know-all, the intellectual secularisation of the eighteenth century did not end in the hyper-critical position of the French, which, from its old connections, it might so easily have done. Scottish intellectuals were only mild reformers of the social and political structure and of property rights. And that middle position is the position from which economic change is not only more likely to come, but, equally important, not to be opposed, to be acceptable. Less speculatively, the Union provided the wider stage, particularly of more rapidly growing markets, in which the entrepreneurial qualities of the Scot could be, and were, successfully played out. But there was a snag, which is related to the apparent slowness with which economic opportunities in Scotland have sometimes been exploited. The entrepreneurial qualities were personal, and their benefits to Scotland were lost when their possessors emigrated. From the time of the Union they did so increasingly: to London, England, the colonies, for the opportunities there were greater still, and so the benefits of the institutional opportunities of the Union for the exercise of entrepreneurial talent were reduced by the opportunities it provided for the possessors to leave Scotland.

Not all left. Enough remained to provide the initiative for economic growth at home; but how? Economic growth required the removal of any restraints of a weak exchange position, possibly through agricultural improvement. The economic argument is reinforced by more general social considerations, which required landowners above all others to accept the inevitability, and preferably the desirability, of economic growth, even if they did not provide the initiative for it themselves; for they were the unquestioned leaders of Scottish society at the time of the Union. The end of an effective Scottish administration, with the abolition of the Scottish parliament and privy council, increased the need for the landowners to use their power and influence in favour of economic growth, for their social prestige was matched by their political power, as heritors, justices of the peace, commissioners of supply, and — a point which can easily be forgotten — as members of a range of influential *ad hoc* devices, such as the Board of Trustees. After the Union the evidence is overwhelming that the landowners not only accepted economic change but that they themselves provided the initiative for change in agriculture and elsewhere.

Several explanations of the landlords' initiative may be offered: sometimes complex economic reasons peculiar to an individual proprietor were the determinants; sometimes the precise form then taken followed the incentives or examples provided by the increased contacts with the south after the Union; sometimes statutory enactments made action much easier. But a more general explanation is required of the widespread nature of the movement, and that is to be found in the significance of the way in which the landowners, especially some of the lesser gentry, who were among the most capable of the improvers, added the eighteenth century concepts of rational social improvement to the existing principles of old-fashioned paternalism, which had determined the form of the administration of estates. Their estates were the society they had to transform. They provide early and specific examples of the forces determining Scottish entrepreneurship.

The willingness to accept agricultural improvement among the landed interest was given a notable boost by the recruitment to its ranks of successful merchants, bankers and lawyers many of whom were of landed stock and so were returning to their heritage. Traditional landowners were not easily distinguished from those more recently established. But the infusion of new blood ensured that the economic opportunity and the social prestige offered by landownership were exploited, and so the traditional power of the land-owner was thrown on the side of economic reform. The economic bias of the contemporary urge for social improvement, which could easily and effectively be grafted into the authoritarian old-fashioned paternalism, was strengthened by some of the new landowners. The urge for social improvement was once again expressed materially.

Economic reform came to agriculture, where it was needed most of all, but the landlord's influence was not limited to agricultural change. As some planned villages still bear witness, the landowners were as interested in industrial enterprises, if they remained subordinate to their rural activities. They were disillusioned only later in the eighteenth century, when a rival industrial interest began to challenge their traditional authority and political power. The economic change which they had initiated could not then be arrested. When the great potential of the application of the new technology to industry appeared later in the eighteenth, and especially in the nineteenth century, the same qualities which had encouraged the landlords into new ways in agriculture encouraged others into the industrial ventures which finally brought the old social and political domination of the landed interest to an end. The rational approach to economic enterprise, in which many Scots found self-fulfilment, was channelled into the industrial economy.

The experience was common to much of the Lowlands, though there were exceptions, and the generalisation does not apply in the Highlands, where, whatever other merits it possessed, perpetuation of the old social values — paternalism without the urge for rational improvement — inhibited economic growth. The rejection of the old social values was one reason why the Argyll estates led in the transformation of the eighteenth century, and a similar rejection, by some of those landowners most vilified by subsequent generations for

71

their apparent lack of humanity and social concern, may be explained as an attempt to deal with a difficult economic problem by the highest motives of eighteenth century rationalism. Many of these much criticised Highland landlords were no different from their counter-parts in the Lowlands. They applied the same progressive principles, but what worked in the Lowlands frequently failed in the Highlands.

The exception does not invalidate the main point. At the time of the Union economic growth required change most of all in agriculture, and the new economic order was initiated and fostered by qualities which were frequently indigenous. The impact of the Union neither produced a new economic problem nor a ready-made solution. It merely provided one political framework within which a solution was possible. Hence it is not surprising that the Union's impact on economic growth was not immediate and that the rate of economic growth was slow for at least fifty years thereafter. Later in the century, when the rate of growth accelerated for other reasons, and the economy assumed a more modern structure, any influence of the particular form of political arrangement was of little relevance to that success. But even if the causal impact of the Union on economic growth was but slight, it was still the political framework within which many Scots found full self-expression, satisfaction and success in economic activities. There was a chronological, if not a logical connection between the Union and economic growth, and that was as far as most people took their analysis. It was a connection which led to assimilation as part of Great Britain, and that accorded with the ideas of those who contributed towards the formation of those entrepreneurial qualities which made for success. The great intellectuals of Scotland in the eighteenth century had no doubt that they were anxious to maintain the closest links with England and with Europe. The engineers were not interested in national boundaries. For those at the other end of the social scale, the problems of urban living posed by industrialisation made for assimilation. Life in Glasgow was similar to life in Liverpool, especially if

you were an Irish immigrant in any case. To all such people there seemed little need to consider to what extent the Union may have encouraged economic growth, for there was no doubt that it was accompanied by it, and that was sufficient proof of the pudding for so many.

Different political arrangements might have produced a more rapid rate of economic progress, but from shortly after the Union such counter-factual statements were irrelevant, for it was not easy to compare Scottish economic growth adversely with that in England. The declining economic activities were often in the south. Glasgow cornered the tobacco trade; the old woollen centres gave way to the new cotton centres, in Lanarkshire as well as in Lancashire; shipbuilding moved from the Thames to the Clyde. As Scotland's economic progress was consolidated, there is little contemporary evidence of counter-factual statements of the benefits of alternative political arrangements, such as were to be found immediately after the Union or in the twentieth century. That is hardly surprising. After the Union the objectives of many Scots were increasingly economic; they were satisfied, perhaps, with a mess of pottage, and with that they were certainly being supplied ever more generously after 1707. As long as the supply was maintained, they were satisfied with, or at least disinterested in the political arrangements. Hence in considering the impact of the Union on economic growth in the widest sense, it is less significant to stress the effect of the Union on economic growth than the effect of economic growth on the Union. The Union assisted but did not cause economic growth: economic growth made the Union acceptable.

NOTES

1. *The letters of David Hume,* ed. J.Y.T. Greig (Oxford 1932), i (1766—76), p. 264.
2. Sir James Steuart, *An Inquiry into the Principles of Political Economy,* ed. A.S. Skinner (Edinburgh 1966), i, p. 324. See also i, pp. 516—17.
3. A. Smith, *The Wealth of Nations,* ed. E. Cannan (London 1904), i, pp. 281f and 221—2.

4. See pp. 33—6.
5. For details see R.H. Campbell, *Scotland since 1707* (Oxford 1965), pp. 56—7.
6. See p. 34.
7. Steuart, *Political Economy*, ii, p. 514.
8. SRO, Customs records. R/20 and RH 2/4.
9. Steuart, *Political Economy*, ii, p. 517.
10. T.S. Ashton, *Economic Fluctuations in England 1700—1800* (Oxford 1959), p. 173.
11. Smith, *Wealth of Nations*, i, p. 84, Smith later tested his proposition by examining the statistics of the manufacture of linen in Scotland. He examined the connection between dearth and difficulties in manufacturing and considered it was proved in 1740 but not in 1756, when dearth was accompanied by 'more than ordinary advances' in Scottish linen production. In 1756, however, the trade was given an extraordinary stimulus through the restoration of export bounties.
12. British Parliamentary Papers, 1803—4, vii, pp. 487 and 507.
13. SRO, Customs records. R/20 and RH 2/4.
14. Dugald Stewart, Dissertations Exhibiting the Progress of Metaphysical, Ethical and Political Philosophy Since the Revival of Letters in Europe. *Collected Works*, ed. Hamilton (Edinburgh 1854—60), i, p. 550.

Scottish Agriculture and the Union: An Example of Indigenous Development

A FENTON MA BA

Assistant Keeper, National Museum of Antiquities of Scotland

Historical truth, like any other truth, varies for every observer according to his personal background and training. For this reason it is hard to believe in absolutes; but nevertheless it is necessary to get as close to the truth, to the realities of an historical situation, as human ingenuity in exploring sources will permit. The problems of interpretation increase as we move back in time and sources grow scantier, but one of the great problems remains that of the personal element ensuing from the learned apparatus, upbringing, and affiliations of the researcher. In the word of John Galt's *Provost*:

'In their [these] notandums, I have endeavoured, in a manner, to be governed by the spirit of the times in which the transaction happened; for I have lived long enough to remark that if we judge of past events by present motives, and do not try to enter into the spirit of the age when they took place, and to see them with the eyes with which they were really seen, we shall conceit many things to be of a bad and wicked character that were not thought so harshly of by those who witnessed them, nor even by those who, perhaps, suffered from them'.[1]

The aim, therefore, in these notes on agriculture before and at the time of the Union of Scotland and England in 1707, is not to prejudge any issues under the influence of knowledge of later improvements and writings, but simply to try to let the conditions of the period speak for themselves.

Although the fact that agriculture is basic to the understanding of Scotland has been emphasised by historians,[2] neither the actual nature of that agriculture, nor its regional variations, has been studied in the kind of depth that permits other than more or less generalised statements which fail to get right down to the regional realities. This situation can only be remedied by a great deal of patient study of printed and manuscript sources, of culling and collocating innumerable details till they begin to form patterns. Above all, it is a primary necessity to carry out a series of closely detailed studies of pre-1750 agriculture in a set of carefully selected regions.

Professor Gordon Donaldson has already reviewed the most rewarding sources available — cartularies, Exchequer Rolls, testamentary records, court books, estate papers, the Registers of the Great Seal and of the Privy Council, the Acts of the Parliament of Scotland, and so on.[3] Not the least interesting of the points that arise in setting together the data from such sources is the way in which the ordinances of the central authority are seen being applied at local level in the court books, for example in relation to the planting of trees and certain types of crops, the prohibition of muirburn, etc. Many of these Acts[4] were repeated time and again at both national and local levels — a clear indication of the difficulties of enforcement. Equally interesting is the fact that sources such as court books reflect so little of national politics and warfare, and no one can easily guess from them which were the years of dearth and which of plenty.

Some of such sources have already been used in several printed discussions of the infield-outfield organisation and cropping patterns, especially in relation to the eighteenth century, e.g. by Symon, Handley, Campbell, Smout and others. These details, therefore, need not be repeated here.[5]

Although the late seventeenth and early eighteenth centuries were still far from the days of real improvement, nevertheless a context for practical advance was being laid down, the result of a long series of changes and modifications, often in themselves minute, often enforced by the simple fact of the wearing out of the resources — peat, turf, grazing, timber — whose interlocking in the daily economy made community existence possible.

This latter point can be readily exemplified with

reference to patterns of settlement and land use. In 1684, there were to be seen the ruins of an old 'town' called Rattra in the parish of Borgue, Kirkcudbright. Here there 'was of old kept a weekly market; but the town is long since demolished, and near the ruins thereof is now a little village, which yet retaines the name of the old town'.[6] It is probable that movement of this kind was not uncommon, as sources of fuel in particular wore out, especially in areas where the economic basis was pastoral rather than arable. It was not difficult to re-site buildings constructed of little more than sods and thatch, with the necessary roofing timbers, as was shown much later during the clearances in the Highlands; but movement was much harder where the township's economy depended on good infield land, and the houses and buildings formed a close-knit functional unit with the arable.

Of a different nature was change due to wood clearance, and extension of the settlement area. Gordon of Straloch, for instance, shows that in north-east Scotland, at least, the nucleated township or joint-farming unit with associated run-rig fields was not as general as many writers have implied. He described how, before 1662, husbandmen were *formerly* gathered in village settlements, to each of which as much land was allotted as could be tilled by four ploughs. This area, the *daach* or *davoch*, works out on a legal calculation based on a Court of Exchequer calculation of 1585 at four ploughgates of 104 acres each, i.e. 416 acres, though this was no doubt a legal rather than an actual extent. Strathbogie was formerly divided into forty village settlements or davochs, and Gordon noted that though in the higher lying districts the davoch boundaries still remained, nevertheless reorganisation had been carried out by the proprietors because, the woods having been cut down, four ploughs were no longer enough to work the area. The lands were therefore divided so that the settlements became continuous, not contiguous, i.e. clustered settlement became dispersed. Gordon saw instances of the procedure in his early years, when the farmers abandoned the villages and removed each to his possession, establishing a new home where any vein of rich soil attracted him. This was a matter of his own choice — not the laird's. In Gordon's day, every plough was drawn by four or five yokes of oxen, and since the number of ploughs had doubled, a considerable acreage of ground was required. All woods had been cut down, and all the land where there was hope of a crop made over to tillage.[7] He saw here the completion of a process of settlement expansion, no doubt one of many that in the late seventeenth century was taking Scottish farming to its cultivation limits, mirroring population growth on the one one hand, at least in this district, and on the other hastening the using up of the resources about whose conservation the Court Books are so vociferous. Amongst the initial results must have been a regional worsening in the level of individual subsistence, for which there was no possibility of permanent amelioration for a century and more to come.

In pre-Reformation times change was equally an indigenous part of the Scottish landscape, sometimes in ways that ran counter to the clustered settlement concept. For example, the granges of Coupar and Aberbothrie were leased to tenants in 1473, each tenant being given his own farm on which he had to build a house. The fenced corn-fields were sown and harvested in joint-occupation, and the meadows and pastures fenced so that each tenant had his own pasture. This was a kind of inverted form of the present-day crofting system, in which the arable was held in common and the grazing subdivided, instead of vice versa. It would be interesting to know if such changes meant anything in terms of movement of cottars and it may be significant that about the same period, 1469–73, the Abbey of Coupar formed a village of about a hundred cottars, each with one to three acres, at Balgersho – a village which by 1492 had grown and prospered and become the burgh of barony of Keithick for Coupar Abbey, possessing a corn mill, waulk mill, common alehouse, and several hostelries.[8] The establishment of the village can be interpreted as an attempt to avoid over-crowding of the farming land whilst yet maintaining in the vicinity a large reservoir of manpower of the kind it was essential to have during harvest, the peak of the farming year, when far more people were required during a three to four week period, for shearing and binding the crop, than it would

have been possible for any single family unit to maintain on
an all-the-year round basis.

By the time of the Union, therefore, the existing set of
forms of land use, especially those with an arable rather than
a pastoral emphasis, was beginning to burst at the seams
through having reached the limits of expansion and through
the using up of resources for fuel, building and manure.
There is evidence for this even in our most northerly islands,
already at a much earlier date, for it was noted in Shetland in
1597 that 'of late the labourers attempted to manure farther
within the country than their predecessors were accustomed
to do, but they reported small advantage for their pains'.[9]

The first positive signs of new directions were indicated
by the publication of writings on agricultural topics, though
these were little more than a trickle in relation to the flood
of political pamphleteering that swirled around the Union.

The earliest pamphlet directly concerned with
agricultural improvement is probably Archibald Napier's 'The
New Order of Gooding and Manuring of all Sorts of Field
Land with Common Salts',[10] the first part of which deals
with salt as a manure, and the second with an intricate system
of fields or enclosures for dunging the land. This appeared in
1595 and bears the experimental imprint of a man who got
married at fifteen and was the son of the inventor of
logarithms.

Over sixty years later, some time about 1666, John
Skene of Hallyards wrote his 'Manuscript of Husbandrie'.[11]
He described the farming system in his parish of Kirkliston,
Midlothian, with its cropping sequences of bere, oats, wheat
and pease, repeated *ad infinitum* on the 'croft land', and of
three successive crops of oats on the outfield, after it had lain
uncropped for two to four years, with the use of folded
animals to manure it before cropping. Cattle were equally
important, for fattening and milk production as well as for
draught. Oxen for grazing were bought for example in
Dunblane on Whitsunday Monday and doubled in value by
Martinmas. Milk cows were bought in Edinburgh on Trinity
Monday, after Whitsun, and oxen, cows, queys, stirks, young
stots, and horses were purchased at Linlithgow on Magdalen

day, nine days before Lammas. There was, therefore, a well
established network of quite far-flung supply centres for the
area's various needs in farm-stock, similar to that described
by Andrew Symson for Galloway. Furthermore the spring
buying and autumn selling of oxen fattened on the summer's
grass was pointing towards a money rather than a subsistence
economy.

Manure was applied before wheat and especially before
bere, but what is of considerable importance as a step
towards improvement was the application of lime before
pease on the croftland or infield. The stress is on the infield,
not the pease. Even by this date, the 1660s, however, liming
was no new phenomenon in the Lothians. It is well
documented in the Parish Reports for 1627 in several parts of
East and Mid Lothian, and in Ayrshire there are references
dating from 1604 and 1616.[12] The principles of its use in
sweetening sour, acid soils were not necessarily properly
understood, however, for its wrong or excessive application
can kill the plant and animal life, producing barren areas;
this had been learned by bitter experience already by 1626.[13]
If the lime level is wrong, heavy manuring will not produce
good crops, but if the lime is right and the manure good,
yields go up immediately. Around the Union period, lime was
mostly applied to the *outfield,* before *oats.* It was in fact an
important aid to the more frequent and more extensive
cropping of the outfield with oats, helping to speed up and
push on the equation of the outfield land, and providing a
basis for the marked rent increases of the Lothians, for
example. The outfield conversion process accelerated after
the Union, and it was often on the outfield area that the
single farms — the Einzelhöfe — of the improvement
agriculture of later days were first established.

Short as it is, Skene's Manuscript contains several useful
pointers, and, in addition, he earmarks regional variation in
types of dairy farming when he writes that:

'Kys milk is best for butter, and yows milk best for
cheiss, for kys milk will give both more butter and better
butter than yows milk, and yows milk will give both mor
cheiss and better cheiss than kys milk. They use in

Cuninghame to make cheiss of kys milk, but it is not good.'[14]

The dairying emphases of south-west Scotland, it seems, were already well known before the Union.

Whereas Skene's Manuscript is factual and practical, the two more substantial treatises that appeared at the very end of the seventeenth century are much more advisory and theoretical. The first of these was James Donaldson's *Husbandry Anatomiz'd,* in 1697. Donaldson, an Edinburgh printer and journalist, says he spent his first twenty years on the land, but his treatise is heavily influenced by earlier English agricultural writers, especially Gervase Markham who himself borrowed from German as well as English sources. The material is not localised and there is no real assessment of an actual situation as a foil against which to set his somewhat bookish proposals for improvement. His recommendations for the use of lime as an element in compost dunghills of old thatch, clay turf, dung and straw, to be laid on the outfield, may be noted, along with those for the growing of potatoes as a field crop,[15] but the chief value of the work is less in relation to practical farming, than as a pointer to the spirit of the age that could inspire an essentially literary man to write in this way, on the analogy of the several earlier English agricultural authors.

Two years later, published in Edinburgh in 1699, there appeared *The Countrey-Man's Rudiments, or An Advice to the Farmers in East Lothian how to Labour and Improve their Ground,* by ABC, thought to have been John Hamilton, the second Lord Belhaven. This is a far more practical piece of work, which, though written primarily to help 'ordinary Farmers', is also aimed at encouraging in agricultural improvements the nobility who are rather inclined to follow 'the old trodden Path to *London'*. Here is a Jacobite suggesting that it was good to work for a living, rather than to depend solely on court patronage. Belhaven seeks to base his advice on the actual conditions in East Lothian, where the soil was amongst the best in Scotland.

As in Skene's Midlothian notes, the infield cropping was a four-break sequence of pease, wheat, barley and oats. Belhaven proposed a five-break sequence, to include an additional crop of pease, with *fauching* or fallowing of part of the two breaks for pease. This he shrewdly saw as a relatively painless way to solve the problem of breaking the prejudice against fallowing on the infield. It was perhaps hardly surprising that farmers should have been unwilling to fallow when they needed all the grain they could get, not only for themselves and their stock, but to pay part of their servants' wages and also — a matter of great importance in dictating the extent and nature of the crops — for paying the rent. Belhaven's contemporary, Andrew Fletcher of Saltoun, put this point very strongly when he said in one of his *Discourses:*

'The Rent being altogether in Corn, the Grounds must be altogether in Tillage; which has bin the ruin of all the best Countries in Scotland'.[16]

However, fallowing was not an unknown phenomenon in Scotland. It was a normal part of the outfield practice, the term being used of that part of the outfield left untilled until it gathered strength again. There is also some scanty evidence, which needs to be strengthened, for infield fallow, e.g. a reference was made to 'wheat fauche' in the Melrose area in 1673, and wheat appears always to have been an infield crop. [17]

In this respect, therefore, some pre-Union stirrings of improvement can be pinpointed, but their importance must not be over-estimated, for still in 1729 Mackintosh of Borlum was saying that 'some of the Gentlemen think that fallow can never be of profit', though others, such as General Ross, Laird of Balnagowan, were imposing summer fallow on their tenants.[18] Mackintosh, like Belhaven, stressed the need for fallow on the infield, on the best third of the land, to keep up its heart.[19]

The proper and widespread use of lime was also very much part of Belhaven's philosophy. On the question of enclosing, however, little was said, except in relation to folds and to parks for grazing cattle and horses. It was, of course, the spread of this type of grazing enclosure that led to the Levellers' Revolt in Galloway in 1724, in an area where cattle played a pre-eminent part in the economy. In 1705 when Joseph Taylor journeyed to Edinburgh, he noted that the

country around the town was all open, abounding with oats, but that 'the meadow ground hereabouts is very inconsiderable, it's generally enclos'd with a mud or stone wall, and goes by the name of a park, but is rather a pasture for cattle, and according to the Reputation of these parks, they set a price upon the Cattle which come from them, those we saw containing but few acres of ground'.[20] The enclosing of arable, however, was still and for long remained a rarity, hardly considered by Belhaven, and first discussed at length in the Scottish agricultural literature by that apostle *par excellence* of enclosing, the Jacobite Mackintosh of Borlum, whose *Essay* was written for the good of his country whilst he languished far from the soil in his Edinburgh jail, turning his sword into a ploughshare.

Generally speaking, the period of arable enclosure in East Lothian occurred between 1730 and 1790, with appropriate time lags in the less advanced parts of the country. English travellers of the Union period and earlier were astonished at the unenclosed landscape; according to Thomas Kirk of Crookrig, a blunt and scurrilous Yorkshireman, 'they are freed from the charge and incumbrance of Enclosures, the whole being but one large Waste, surrounded with the Sea'.[21] In the long run, however, the English enclosures certainly had an effect in Scotland, and people like Thomas, sixth Earl of Haddington, about 1735, went so far as to import a farmer from Dorset, 'in hopes that he would instruct my people in a right way of inclosing'.[22]

For the Union period, therefore, arable enclosure was not part of the scene. The only enclosures were fold dykes, mostly of turf since they were not necessarily permanent fixtures, and yard, garden or orchard dykes, park dykes, and tree plantation dykes, which could be of stone when associated with big houses, as at Urie in 1701, 'the deike being sufficiently coped with stones'.[23] Turf or feal was the main dyke building material, for, as Mackintosh of Borlum pointed out, not only was stone and lime enclosure very expensive, but a stone wall never improved — it was starting to deteriorate from the day of its erection; hedges, on the other hand, were improving all the time, if well looked after.[24]

Some other points in the *Countrey-Man's Rudiments* deserve annotation. Just as the nature of the infield-outfield system with its run-rig form (whether fixed or periodic) made fallowing and indeed enclosure difficult without a major reorganisation, so also was it difficult to introduce cultivated grass. Grass was a great rarity in East Lothian amongst the husbandmen, 'neither can they well have it (as at present their Farmes are ordered) unless they turn some part of their infield Land into Grass, and lime as much of their outfield Land as correspondes thereto'.[25] Indeed, Lord Haddington's Dorset pace-setters, who tried to teach grass-seed management as well as enclosing, found themselves faced with considerable opposition. Why should a man sow grass on land that could carry corn? It is not the least interesting facet of the history of the period that the superimposition of ideas of improvement, whether in relation to cultivated grass, fallowing, or enclosure — in so far as these affected the infield organisation — did, in fact, stir up opposition amongst the country folk, though rarely on the scale of the Levellers. There is no doubt, however, that when the period of improvement set in firmly, it was always easier for the first inroads to be made in the outfield and commons. Potatoes (which in Belhaven's time were, with turnips, only a garden crop) made a good accompaniment to this method of approach, for they were an excellent cleaning agent on newly reclaimed land and gave good returns.

Belhaven also gave us the first consistent description of an ideal farm-building layout. It must partly reflect something of the building policy on the biggest and best farms of the period, but did not become general for another seventy years or more. Instead of a line or random cluster of buildings, he advocated a four-square formation around a central yard containing the midden. Farm-houses have moved away from the midden now, but in 1699 this was advanced thinking.

These agricultural writings by landed gentry and a literate printer surely reflect something of the contemporary preoccupation, even obsession, with trade and economics to the extent that their authors, by writing as they do, bring into prominence the problems Scottish agriculture had to face in making its transition to a money-based system, matching that of England and many other parts of Europe. But, alongside the purely rural farming organisation of the estates, there was also the town or burgh farming that integrated closely with trade and small-scale industry and was controlled by the councils of burgesses rather than directly by lairds. The 'agrarian aspect of municipal life',[26] deserves close study, for not only is the way in which town and country mingled of great fascination in itself, but also it seems that the seeds of improvement, perhaps forced on by population pressure, were germinating earlier in and around the towns than in the open country. This is a thesis that remains to be developed, but one or two examples may be given at the moment. Reclamation of moorland was certainly of importance, for in Lanark, on 14 July 1659, the part of the muir called the Meadowhill was rouped and set by the Council for a thirteen year period,

'the first yeir to lyme and fauch without payment, the nixt four to be corne and to pay the yeirlie deutie, the nixt tua yeir to lie for the cattell without payment, the nixt tua to be corne and to pay, the nixt tua to lie for the cattell, and the last tua to be corne and to pay the yeirlie deutie'.[27] This was, for the time, an enlightened policy.

In Kirkintilloch, too, the 'mettstares' were active from at least the 1650s, measuring land so that it could be allocated for individual use, as in 1670 when the Baillies ordained that the Gartcosh land 'shall be dealt and coutchit to everie màn his owne pairt and coutch', on condition that manure deficiences should be made up.[28] This and several other examples from the same source seem to indicate a blocking-out or lotting of holdings into self-contained units.

But this is nothing to do with the Union; rather is it an indigenous development whose diffusion, if any, beyond the burgh limits remains to be investigated. Of a more exogenous nature, however, more directly a product of the intellectual fever generated by Union thinking, was the proposal made by an unknown writer to the Duke of Atholl in 1708, to set up a new town at Logierait, near the junction of the Tay and the Tummel in Perthshire.[29] The writer says that though his ideas had been put together several years before, he had waited to hear the result of the Union proposals before putting them forward, 'and fynding hapily that Supperiorities and here[11] (heritable) offices were reserved as before I was thereby inclined to resume my purpose'. This is a clear acknowledgment of the writer's consciousness of the importance of heritable jurisdictions for centralised control in a context where the people could do little or nothing for themselves. His inspiration was the flourishing state of the trade in Perth in cattle, wethers, plaiding, linen, bark and timber, all the produce of the rural hinterland for which the town provided an outlet and thereby a stimulus. His proposals, briefly, were to establish a weekly court and market at Logierait for the Regality of Atholl, with particular days for the sale of ewes, lambs, and new calved and farrow cows, for wethers, for oxen and fat cattle, for horses, linen, woollen cloth, etc.; to establish a group of town officers; to provide for the education of youth, with free schools for the poor; to improve the quality of the sheep's wool for the women to spin by destroying the numerous foxes, so that the sheep no longer needed to be housed at night, a practice that had made them small and degenerate; to develop the growing of lint for spinning, and to introduce the lint wheel to replace the distaff; to improve the weaving, if necessary by bringing expert weavers from the south, and expanding the industry up to 500 weavers with their apprentices; to exploit the timber in the Regality carefully and professionally, not allowing the husbandmen to work it any longer for their houses, house plenishing and horse graith, wasting three times more than they needed; to train maltmen properly for brewing, their skill at that time being low or non-existent, and to control the sale of victual both for food and for brewing (the writer disapproved of excessive drinking and of the custom of standing drinks); to establish mills for grinding grain and milling cloth; and in general to keep going a whole range of craftsmen and tradesmen — masons, wrights, skinners, bonnetmakers, candlemakers, baxters, smiths, shoemakers, tailors, weavers, not to mention barbers and apothecaries. The concept of the provision of crafts and services seems remarkably modern. No new town was established, however, although a new courthouse was built; but the document itself remains as a monument to the spirit of the age, and is of value for the quite considerable light it sheds on this Highland-line community. Its proposals are completely in keeping with the rapid contemporary spread of marketing centres, this itself being an indication of improving conditions, for markets are useless without produce to sell.

In reviewing the early sources that have a specific bearing on agriculture, what stands out most strongly is the tightly-knit nature of the infield area, physically and socially. In itself this was one of the main impediments to progress, much more so than the conservatism of the lairds. The 1695 Enclosure Acts removed any legal barriers to run-rig enclosure, but such enclosure involved the uprooting of a working settlement pattern, and the mass movement of people. It could not, however, involve the loss of people, for how could the laird face the harvest without workers? — who would cut and carry his winter fuel? — who would plough his rigs? For a system heavily if not entirely dependent on services, this was a crucial point. Seasonal needs required a surplus of people, who were self-supporting by their individual small stakes in the soil and stock, and who, by providing services in lieu of rents, permitted very cheap running of the Mains farm with almost no cash commitments. The removal of this surplus of people would mean that the laird, tacksman or tenant farmer would be forced to think of digging into his pocket in order to pay for extra seasonal help. Accordingly, the destruction of the nodal infield organisation could be not undertaken lightly unless some supply of capital was available to the landowners, for example, through trade and industry, and one aspect of this was the development of marketing centres, the establishment of planned villages, especially of weavers, and the rapid contemporary growth of the main towns.

The infield area must not be regarded as complete in

itself. For its integrated working the outfield, the moor grazings, and in some areas the shielings, were also essential. If one of these elements was cut off, the organism became imperfect and the balance was upset. This imbalance had occurred earlier when liming brought outfield areas up to infield standards, without the accompaniment of infield fallow, sown grass, etc., which would have allowed for the production of surplus fodder for the maintenance of the stock of those whose employment was mainly seasonal, the outfield grazings having ceased to be available.

The social situation that was essential to the maintenance of the system is brought into focus by an examination of the work organisation of the plough.

In 1666 John Forbes, the Aberdeen printer, included in his volume of *Cantus, Songs and Fancies* a three-part polyphonic song called the Pleugh-Song. Its origins may go back to around 1600, but its description of the plough, team, and manpower apply just as readily to one hundred years later. Though unlocalised, it provides a vivid glimpse of a Lowland form of community organisation.

The plough was of wood, apart from the iron share, coulter, and bridle to which the draught was attached; it had two handles, and was drawn by a team of eight oxen each of which had its own descriptive name.

Twenty-five workers are referred to by name in one text, and twenty-one in another, some of the names, such as *mawer* and *tasker,* suggesting their jobs. Since the minimum manpower required for the plough teams of the period was two, one man between the stilts guiding the plough, the other controlling and urging on the animals with goad, stick, or whip, the Pleugh-Song numbers are clearly excessive. Some would be required for the operations that accompanied ploughing, such as harrowing and sowing, but the majority, as tenants or sub-tenants in the *farm-town,* may have had a direct stake in the plough and its equipment. Since according to an Act of James I in 1424 every man of simple estate who worked as a labourer should have half an ox in the plough, or else should dig with the spade a specified area each work day, it was theoretically possible for an eight-ox plough team to have sixteen owners, each with a half share in an ox.[30] Neighbouring of this kind continued in places until the nineteenth century, though the inconstancy of human nature is underlined by entries such as one for 1678 in the *Forbes Baron Court Book:*

'William Menie in Castell Forbes sall stryk oxen in a plewch with James Duncain, and sall bear good neighbourhood with him'.[31]

In the work team of the Pleugh-Song, there is an impression of the camaraderie, movement, and sound of voices that may still be sometimes seen in parts of Central Europe, when the villagers are out in force on the fields, working hard, but by no means oppressed by their tasks. Similarly at harvest time, it is possible to imagine the bustle on the rigs, women shearing with the sickle, men binding sheaves and stooking, inservants, outservants, neighbours, extra hands from the cot-towns, villages and towns, members of the family of all ages, all joining in this urgent task.

The plough-team can also be used to index some of the broader patterns of Scottish agriculture. The plough of the Pleugh-Song was the so-called old Scotch plough, the primary implement of Lowland agriculture until late in the eighteenth century. Though horses were also used to pull it, oxen, or a mixture of horses and oxen, arranged two by two, in line ahead, were its normal means of traction. This is reflected in the legal terminology, for the *oxgang* was a unit of land based on the working capabilities of each of a team of eight oxen, an eighth of a plough-gate.

But in the Highlands and Islands of Scotland (excluding Shetland and in part Orkney), in parts of Galloway, in Ireland and the Isle of Man, the ubiquitous draught animal was the horse, yoked as a rule in teams of four abreast. To such an extent was this built into the system, that in north Scotland, Perth, Argyll, Angus and Lanark the unit of land measurement was the *horsegang,* reckoned as the amount of land allotted to each of a team of four horses, a fourth part of a plough-gate. The term goes back to 1720, but is implied in the expression 'four horse plough-gang' recorded in 1640.[32]

It can usually be assumed that differences reflected in

this way in the legal terminology are fundamental. The implements also varied, for in the Highlands and Islands more than one variety of single-stilted plough was in use, whose antecedents go back to prehistory, and on the Highland line a lighter version of the old Scotch plough, with a pair of very upright stilts, was to be found. There is a clear dichotomy here between the Highlands and Lowlands, and the impression is given that the heavy plough with its team of eight oxen or more intruded and spread, probably along with feudalism, displacing the plough types and teams more akin to the Highland survivors.

By the Union period, there was a variety of cultivating implement types in Scotland, whether drawn by animals or operated by the human hand and foot. These, though crude and clumsy as seen through the eyes of the 'improving' writers of the late eighteenth and nineteenth centuries, had nevertheless evolved over a long period of time to a state of sophisticated adaptation to their environmental conditions. The size and nature of the team, the techniques of cultivation and the associated fields or lazy-beds, evolved continuously and unspectacularly along with the implement types, as part and parcel of the set of socio-agrarian systems within which they occurred. Until the Union and for many years afterwards, this was a purely indigenous form of evolution, on which the Union made no immediate impact.

It is possible and indeed likely that by the time of the Union, the old system had been driven as far as it could go in several areas, due to population growth, the using up of resources in fuel, and the limitation of further settlement expansion. There was a need for new directions, some of which had already begun to appear within the existing system. The outstanding example is the cattle trade of the south-west and of the Lothians, leading to special grazing requirements and thence to grazing enclosures. Even in the Highlands, the Lowland demand for cattle had its effect, not only in the establishment of fairs, as at Portree in Skye in 1580, but also in changing the traditional period of the return from the shielings, which had to be before harvest to accommodate the needs of the drovers who wanted cattle for the Falkirk and Stenhousemuir Fairs in mid-September. In this way, economic incentives were able to bring about an adaptation of the transhumant system, well before the Union.

Possibly the cattle trade also played as much of a part as cropping requirements in stimulating the use of lime on the outfield, for better grass could give a better carrying capacity for animals. On the arable, better crops and more straw, allied to a slow increase in the amount of hay made, meant that greater numbers of stock could be overwintered.

The use of lime as a fertiliser began over a century before alterations, which are still only being foreshadowed in the writings of Donaldson and Belhaven, began to be imposed on the crops and cropping sequences in the infield. Here much less flexibility was possible, and change had to be of a more exogenous nature, that is, it had to be firmly imposed on an existing system which was broken up in the process. If the Union had any real impact on Scottish agriculture, it was by providing further economic incentives, and by making Scottish landowners more aware of earlier and current improvements in England. The developments in the pastoral and to a lesser degree in the arable sectors that had started long before and that ran through the Union period were primarily indigenous. The Union ultimately helped to make the leaders of agriculture society in Scotland more aware of a wider and more capitalistic world, and this new awareness began to be reflected in terms of land use, enclosure, and implement types three or four decades after the Union. The imposition of exogenous factors like arable enclosures and rotations, with root crops and sown grasses, involved a far-reaching remodelling of the socio-agrarian structure and settlement pattern, but this was almost entirely post-Union. Though some developments are adumbrated before the Union and were intensified after it, it is scarcely possible to speak in terms of 'the impact of the Union' on the agriculture of the period.

NOTES

1. John Galt, *The Provost* [1822] (London and Edinburgh 1913), pp. 172–3.
2. Cf. G.G. Coulton, *Scottish abbeys and social life* (Cambridge 1933), p. 134.
3. G. Donaldson, 'Sources for Scottish agrarian history before the eighteenth century', *Agricultural History Review [Agric. H.R.]* viii (2) (1960), pp. 82–90.
4. Listed in J.A. Symon, *Scottish farming past and present* (Edinburgh and London 1959), pp. 453–5.
5. J.A. Symon, op. cit.; J.E. Handley, *Scottish farming in the eighteenth century* (London 1953); J.E. Handley, *The agricultural revolution in Scotland* (London 1963); R.H. Campbell, *Scotland since 1707: the rise of an industrial society* (Oxford 1965); T.C. Smout, *A history of the Scottish people, 1560–1830* (London 1969); A. Fenton, 'The rural economy of East Lothian in the 17th and 18th century', in *Transactions of the East Lothian Antiquarian and Field Naturalists' Society*, ix (1963).
6. A. Symson, *A large description of Galloway, 1684* (Edinburgh 1823), p. 25.
7. W. Macfarlane, *Geographical collections relating to Scotland*, ed. A. Mitchell, SHS (Edinburgh 1906–8), ii, pp. 272–3, 275–6.
8. *Rental book of the Cistercian abbey of Cupar-Angus*, ed. C. Rogers, Grampian Club (London 1879–80), i, p. 118; T. Bedford Franklin, *A history of Scottish farming* (London 1952), pp. 71f.
9. J. Monipennie, *Certain matters concerning the realmes of Scotland* [1597] (London 1603), p. 9.
10. Printed in *Archaeologia Scotica*, ii (1822), pp. 154–8.
11. A. Fenton, 'Skene of Hallyard's Manuscript of Husbandrie', *Agric. H.R.*, xi (2) (1963), pp. 67–70.
12. T.C. Smout and A. Fenton, 'Scottish agriculture before the improvers – an exploration', *Agric. H.R.*, xiii (2) (1965), pp. 82–4.
13. *Reports on the state of certain parishes in Scotland*, ed. A. Macgrigor, Maitland Club (Edinburgh 1835), p. 44.
14. A. Fenton, 'Skene of Hallyard', p. 69.
15. J. Donaldson, *Husbandry anatomiz'd; or an enquiry into the present manner of teiling and manuring the ground in Scotland* (Edinburgh 1697), pp. 117–20.
16. A. Fletcher, *Two discourses concerning the affairs of Scotland* (Edinburgh 1698), p. 37.
17. *Selections from the records of the Regality of Melrose*, ed. C.S. Romanes, SHS (Edinburgh 1914–17), ii, p. 324.

18. W. Mackintosh, *An essay on ways and means of inclosing, fallowing, planting, etc., in Scotland* (Edinburgh 1729), pp. xxix, xlvi.
19. Ibid., p. 40.
20. J. Taylor, *A journey into Edenborough in Scotland* [1705] (Edinburgh 1903), p. 99.
21. T. Kirk, *A modern account of Scotland; being an exact description of the country and a true character of the people and their manners* (London 1679), p. 4.
22. Earl of Haddington, *Short Treatise on forest trees* (Edinburgh 1756), p. 39.
23. *Court book of the Barony of Urie in Kincardineshire, 1604–1747*, ed. D.G. Barron, SHS (Edinburgh 1829), p. 111.
24. W. Mackintosh, op. cit., pp. xlix, l–li.
25. ABC [Lord Belhaven], *The countrey-man's rudiments, or an advice to the farmers in East Lothian how to labour and improve their ground* (Edinburgh 1699), p. 22.
26. *Court book of the Burgh of Kirkintilloch, 1658–1694*, ed. G.S. Pryde, SHS (Edinburgh 1963), p. lxx.
27. *Extracts from the records of the Royal Burgh of Lanark, 1150–1722*, ed. R. Renwick, Scottish Burgh Record Society (Glasgow 1893), p. 173.
28. *Kirkintilloch Court Bk*, p. 19.
29. J. Munro, 'New town – old style', in *Clan Donnachaidh Annual*, 1969, pp. 37–39; Edinburgh University Library MS. Dc 1.37.1/3.
30. A. Fenton, 'The plough-song: a Scottish source for medieval plough history', *Tools and Tillage*, i (3) (1970), p. 181.
31. 'The Forbes Baron court book', ed. J.M. Thomson, in *Miscellany III*, SHS (Edinburgh 1919), p. 318.
32. A. McKerral, 'Ancient denominations of agricultural land', in *Proceedings of the Society of Antiquaries of Scotland*, lxxvii (1943–4), pp. 53–4.

Patriotic Publishing as a Response to the Union

I S ROSS MA BLitt PhD

Associate Professor of English, University of British Columbia

S A C SCOBIE MA PhD

Assistant Professor of English, University of Alberta

'I'm perswaded, if Scotchmen would often and seriously
reflect upon [the Happy State from which the Kingdom of
Scotland was fall'n], and the Glorious and Heroick Actions
of their Progenitors, it could not fail of Exciting in them a
generous Resolution of Recovering what was so Valiantly
Defended and Maintain'd by their Predecessors, and meanly
parted with by this Age: And I can never suffer myself to
despond or doubt, but that, some time or other, God will
bless such Resolutions and Endeavours with Success, by
Restoring the Nation to its Ancient Rights and Liberties.'
Thus wrote George Lockhart of Carnwath (1673–1731),
one of the commissioners appointed by Queen Anne to draft
the treaty of Union, but opponent of that measure, in the
preface to an anonymous publication of 1714.[1] It is not too
much to claim that the sentiments expressed by Lockhart
animated to a remarkable degree certain contemporaries
associated with publishing. In particular there came from the
printers James Watson and Robert Freebairn, the scholar
Thomas Ruddiman, and the poet-impresario Allan Ramsay an
array of books which illustrated the pattern of Scotland's
glory, fall, and hoped-for restoration mapped out by the
politician.

Awareness of Scotland's struggle for independence from
England and the later reform of her church was kept alive at
the time of the Union by popular editions of Barbour's

Bruce, Blind Harry's *Wallace,* and the writings of Sir David Lindsay.[2] Walter Scott makes dramatic use of references to these sources of nationalist feeling in one of the exchanges in *Rob Roy* between Bailie Nicol Jarvie and Andrew Fairservice. The Bailie speaks for the economic advantages of the Union: '... There's naething sae gude on this side o' time but it might hae been better, and that may be said o' the Union. Nane were keener against it than the Glasgow folk, wi' their rabblings and their mobs, as they ca' them, now-a-days. But it's an ill wind blaws naebody gude — Let ilk ane roose the ford as they find it — I say, Let Glasgow flourish! whilk is judiciously and elegantly putten round the town's arms, by way of by-word. — Now, since St Mungo catched herrings in the Clyde, what was ever like to gar us flourish like the sugar and tobacco-trade? Will ony body tell me that, and grumble at the treaty that opened us a road west-awa' yonder?'

Andrew Fairservice, who is named after Scotland's patron saint and is something of a spokesman for national consciousness, is concerned about legal issues and the symbols of sovereignty and self-defence: 'it was an unco change to hae Scotland's laws made in England; and ... he wadna for a' the herring-barrels in Glasgow, and a' the tobacco-casks to boot, hae gien up the riding o' the Scots Parliament, or sent awa' our crown, and our sword, and our sceptre, and Mons Meg, to be keepit by thae English pock-puddings in the Tower o' Lunnon. What wad Sir William Wallace, or auld Davie Lindsay hae said to the Union, or them that made it?' (Ch. XXVI)

To be sure, a Bailie Nicol Jarvie actually speaking in this way in 1715 would have been a prophetic voice. Writing to his publisher on 4 April 1760, Adam Smith has the following comment on feeling in Scotland immediately after the Union: 'Nothing ... appears to me more excusable than the disaffection of Scotland at that time. The Union was a measure from which infinite Good has derived to this country. The Prospect of that good, however, must then have appeared very remote and very uncertain. The immediate effect of it was to hurt the interest of every single order of men in the country. The dignity of the nobility was undone by it. The greater part of the Gentry who had been accustomed to represent their own country in its own Parliament were cut out for ever from all hopes of representing it in a British Parliament. Even the merchants seemed to suffer at first. The trade to the Plantations was, indeed, opened to them. But that was a trade which they knew nothing about; the trade they were acquainted with, that to France, Holland and the Baltic, was laid under new embarrassments which almost totally annihilated the two first and most important branches of it. The Clergy too, who were then far from insignificant, were alarmed about the Church. No wonder if at that time all orders of men conspired in cursing a measure so hurtful to their immediate interest. The views of their Posterity are now very different; but those views could be seen by but few of our forefathers, by those few in but a confused and imperfect manner'.[3]

The economic plight of Scotland in 1707 was paralleled by a fragmentation of culture and uncertainty about the direction of creative energy into forms of literary expression. The antecedents to this state of affairs lie in the unsettled state of Scotland in the sixteenth and seventeenth centuries resulting in deep religious and political cleavages. Also, the passing of the court to England in 1603 deprived the country thereafter of a central focus for patronage of the arts and struck a telling blow against the use of Scots as a serious literary language. For Scotsmen of the early eighteenth century, the Latin classics formed the staple of literary education and their religious education was based on an English Bible. At least a century separated them from the old Scots literary language of the makars, and they regarded the Scots they spoke as a dialect split off from the mainstream of English. Publishing in 1707 reflected the general cultural fragmentation. As one social historian of the period reports: 'there were only two respectable printing-presses, both belonging to keen Jacobites, in [Edinburgh]; the other booksellers were Presbyterians who printed atrociously'.[4] The direct association of religion, aesthetics, and politics is typical of the age of the Union. As we shall see, the revival of Scottish poetry and the reissue of works of the national literary heritage in the first decades of the eighteenth century, no less than the struggle over forms of church government in the seventeenth century, were in many respects political manifestations.

Of the two keen jacobites who had respectable printing presses, James Watson (?1664–1722) was the more experienced publisher. His career reflects strong political interests and concern for Scotland's economic situation.[5] His father, also James, was the 'Popish Printer' whom James VII set up in Holyroodhouse in 1686 after a mob had broken into his Grassmarket premises and ill treated his workmen. In 1700 the younger Watson was in trouble with the government of William III for publishing a pamphlet expressing the mounting resentment over the Darien disaster: *The People of Scotland's Groans and Lamentable Complaint Pour'd out before the High Court of Parliament.* Among others was the complaint that for a hundred years, since the union of the crowns, the leaders of Scotland had served England and had treated their own people as enemies. Watson submitted to the Privy Council that he printed *Scotland's Groans* not from 'ill design' but from the necessity of providing for his numerous family, but he touched on dangerous political ground again some five years later by his contribution to the tumult over the hanging of three sailors alleged to be English pirates. There came from his press in Craig's Close a ballad entitled *A Pill for the Pork Eaters, or a Scots lancet for an English Swelling,* which made it clear that the deaths were regarded as revenge for the national humiliation over the Darien scheme:

Then England for its treachery should mourn,
Be forced to fawn, and truckle in its turn:
Scots Pedlars you no longer durst upbraid
And DARIEN should with interest be repaid.[6]

In the same year of 1705, Watson was in further trouble with the Privy Council for his involvement in an attempt to defeat English encroachment on reprinting activities. Among the charges brought against him was one for issuing a pamphlet entitled *Scotland reduced by force of Armes and made a Province of England.*

With some justice Watson was proud of having raised the standard of Scottish printing, whose annals he supplied in a preface to a translation of Jean de la Caille's *History of the Art of Printing* which he published in 1713. While he is not in a position to say much about the incunables,[7] he does pay tribute to the 'excellent Masters' of the sixteenth and early seventeenth centuries. His political bias comes out in the account he gives of the decline in printing in Scotland since the time of the 'Usurper', as he consistently describes Cromwell. With the rebellion against Charles I, the 'Royal Martyr', religion and learning fell into a decay and 'Printing, the faithfull Secretary to Both, underwent the same Fate with them' (p. 9). He describes with indignation the fate of Robert Young, the printer of the beautiful Common Prayer Book of 1639: 'this Good and Great Master was ruin'd by the Covenanters, for doing this Piece of Work, and forc'd to fly the Kingdom' (pp. 9–10). In Cromwell's time, after Young's death, his co-partner as King's Printer in Scotland made over the gift of that office 'to some stationers in *London,* who sent down upon us *Christopher Higgins* and some *English* Servants with him: They printed only some News-Papers and some small Books, and these very ill done too' (p. 10). The fall from the original glory of Scottish printing is expressed with a world of scorn in that phrase: 'sent down upon us'.

A partial recovery of the state of printing occurred about the time of the Restoration of Charles II, but disaster returned when Andrew Anderson and his heirs obtained in 1671 the right of being King's Printer for forty-one years: 'By this Gift the Art of PRINTING in this kingdom got a dead stroke; for by it no Printer could print anything from a Bible to a Ballad without Mr Anderson's Licence' (p. 12). Watson's father had foresight enough and interest to purchase for his son the gift after the expiry of the term of Anderson and his heirs as King's Printer, but surviving as a publisher was difficult for Watson, due to the determination of Anderson's widow to maintain to the end the rights derived from her husband. This formidable lady harrassed contemporary printers through litigation and 'fell Tooth and Nail upon the Booksellers' for carrying stocks of Bibles. She

98

pressed her feud with Watson to the point of accusing him publicly in 1712 of using every opportunity to publish jacobite and popish books. Further litigation followed Watson's assumption of the gift in 1711 in association with Robert Freebairn, the other keen jacobite who had a respectable press, and the Queen's Printer in England, John Baskett. For a time, however, both Freebairn and Baskett defected to Mrs Anderson. In the end, Watson was confirmed in his rights as King's Printer by judgments of the Court of Session and the House of Lords, 1716–18, but Baskett's title to a share of the same office was also established. He exercised his double patent to prevent Watson from selling his Bibles in London. Watson attempted to invoke the equal trading privileges guaranteed by the Union (Art. 4), but the Master of the Rolls confirmed Baskett in his monopoly. Doubtless this decision added fuel to Watson's feelings about the economic injustice suffered by Scotland and further strengthened his stand as a patriotic publisher.

Patriotic feeling found a literary vent in the *Choice Collection of serious and comic Scots poems, both ancient and modern* (1706, 1709, 1711), which is the best-known book associated with Watson's name, principally because hindsight represents it as beginning the eighteenth century revival of Scottish vernacular poetry. (While of literary interest, the editions of *Bruce, Wallace,* and the works of Lindsay, already mentioned as being available during the Union era, were chiefly prized as sources of political or religious feeling. The preface of an edition of Lindsay published at Belfast in 1714 makes this clear in its description of the author: 'a man of such Sincerity and Faithfulness, that he spared not, as well in his satyrical Farses and Plays as in all his other Works, to Enveigh most sharply against the Enormities of the Court and the great Corruption of the Clergy'.) What Watson did in the *Choice Collection* was to put his readers in touch with older and contemporary Scottish poetry that was not generally known, and despite the political overtones of a nationalist demonstration, this above all was a literary event. Furthermore, the retrospective nature of the book, its antiquarian air, even, is characteristic of much in Scottish literature: witness the slogan of that twentieth century revolutionary, Hugh MacDiarmid — 'Not Burns — Dunbar!'

In 'derision and contempt' Chancellor Seafield had said of the closing of the Scottish Parliament that it was the 'end of an auld sang' (DNB). Forward-looking writers such as William Robertson decided that the day of a distinctively Scottish literature was over, as we find in the conclusion to his *History of Scotland* (1759): 'the Union having incorporated the two nations, and rendered them one people, the distinctions which have subsisted for many ages gradually wear away; peculiarities disappear; the same manners prevail in both parts of the island; the same authors are read and admired; the same entertainments are frequented by the elegant and polite; and the same standard of taste and purity in language is established. The Scots, after being placed, during a whole century, in a situation no less fatal to the liberty than to the taste and genius of the nation, were at once put in possession of privileges more valuable than those their ancestors had formerly enjoyed; and every obstruction that had retarded their pursuit, or prevented their acquisition of literary fame, was totally removed'. It was the achievement of Watson and his successors in reviving the vernacular, anachronistically, perhaps against hopeless odds, that they heard the 'auld sang' of Scotland and fought a long rearguard action against the process of assimilation so blandly outlined by Robertson.

A prefatory note to the *Choice Collection* reveals that Watson saw it as a pioneering work in Scots which required some kind of justification. The tone is very much on the defensive: 'As the frequency of Publishing Collections of Miscellaneous Poems in our Neighbouring Kingdoms and States, may, in a great measure, justify an undertaking of this kind with us; so, 'tis hoped, that this being the first of its Nature which has been publish'd in our native *Scots* dialect, the Candid Reader may be the more easily induced through the consideration thereof, to give some Charitable Grains of Allowance, if the Performance come not up to such a Point of Exactness as may please an over nice Palate.' At first sight, what follows appears to be an amazing hodge-podge of ebullient and grave poems in the older Scots tongue, courtly lyrics in a variety of linguistic dresses, and macaronic verse, interspersed with squibs, epigrams, satires, and occasional pieces, all of which suggests a highly fragmented literary culture. The older makars are not represented; there are no ballads; and songs are few, though these do include a version of 'Auld Lang Syne' and 'Lady Anne Bothwel's Balow'. Further analysis, however, brings out the riches of the *Choice Collection.* The first poem is 'Christis Kirk on the Grene', which proved to be a central poem in the Scottish vernacular revival, both for its theme, a rollicking description of a religious festival, and its form — a deft arrangement of long and short lines, with a defiant 'bob' at the end that heightens the fun of the verse. The poem inspired Robert Fergusson's 'Hallow-Fair' and 'Leith Races', as well as a number of poems by Burns, including 'The Holy Fair'. In our time, Robert Garioch has caught its mood and spirit admirably in 'Embro to the Ploy', a mocking tribute to the religion of culture and yet another revival of the older Scottish poetry.

> The haly Kirk's Assemby-haa
> nou fairly coups the creel
> wi Lindsay's Three Estaitis, braw
> devices of the Deil.
> About our heids the satire stots
> like hailstanes till we reel;
> the bawrs are in auld-farrant Scots,
> it's maybe jist as weill,
>> imphm,
> in Embro to the ploy. [8]

The first volume of the *Choice Collection* also contained 'The Life and Death of the Piper of Kilbarchan' by Robert Sempill of Beltrees (?1595–?1668), which re-established the use in Scots of a stanza form whose history goes back at least to the time of the first-known troubadour, Count William IX of Poitiers (1071–1127). Allan Ramsay named it 'standart Habby' after the Kilbarchan piper, and we know it now as the 'Burns stanza'. In this stanza form and of the same mock-elegy type was another poem printed by Watson, 'The Last Words of Bonny Heck, a Famous Greyhound in the Shire of Fife', by William Hamilton of Gilbertfield (c. 1665–1751). This kind of mock-testament from the mouth of an animal set another example for the eighteenth-century vernacular revival, most notably followed in Burn's 'Death and Dying Words of Poor Maillie'. Ramsay and Fergusson favoured the mock-elegy for humans such as ale-wives and college characters.[9]

Another stanza form which came to be revived because Watson drew attention to it was that of Alexander Montgomerie's sixteenth century dream allegory, *The Cherrie and the Slae*. Ramsay picked up its highly intricate pattern in 'The Vision', a patriotic poem of his own composition which he inserted in *The Ever Green* (1724), and passed on to Burns who employed it in the genial 'Epistle to Davie' and the marvellous tone poem that is the opening recitativo of *The Jolly Beggars*.[10] Other poems of merit in Watson's first volume are the Latin-Scots *Polemo-Middinia* by Drummond of Hawthornden and 'Hallow my Fancie' by the precocious William Cleland. Of the riches of the second and third volumes it will suffice to mention Drummond's 'Forth Feasting', the lyrics by Sir Robert Aytoun and the Marquis of Montrose, and Montgomerie's 'Flyting with Polwart'.

In formally presenting the poems of the *Choice Collection* Watson was identifying strands of the national culture that had been forgotten or neglected or allowed to survive in ephemeral ways such as broadsides. To some extent the nation was put in touch with its literary past and possibilities for future developments were revealed. Some of these as the eighteenth century saw them have been mentioned, but it would be reasonable to argue that Watson's book prefigures much in modern Scottish poetry: the polylingual and flyting elements in MacDiarmid, for example, as well as the graceful wit of Norman MacCaig, the lyric intensity of Sydney Goodsir Smith, and, as has been illustrated, the adroit satire of Robert Garioch. Furthermore, in the very idea of a 'choice collection' of poems that juxtapose the 'comic and serious' is there not to be found the quintessence of the art of Ian Hamilton Finlay, who assembles his poems with unerring taste and gives them to the world radiant with meanings grave and gay?

As well as being an anthologist, Watson became editor of the works of two celebrated Scottish writers: Drummond of Hawthornden and Sir George Mackenzie of Rosehaugh. For the Drummond edition (1711), which he prepared with the assistance of Thomas Ruddiman, Watson wrote a preface which gives a careful account of the copy texts. While he praises the poems of Drummond, which 'may be justly compared for Sense, Wit and Language with the best English Poems of that Time', he clearly attaches greater importance to the political writings making their first appearance in print. Provocatively, Watson hopes 'these Papers . . . will still be useful and seasonable: They were written in the Time of the late Troubles, and are very keen against Rebellion, and plainly and evidently demonstrate the bad consequences of it. Our Author was a true TORY, and seriously concern'd about the HEREDITARY RIGHT and MONARCHY: He knew very well by his own Experience and the History of past Times, that there never was Peace or Prosperity in the Nation, when that was not inviolably observ'd'.

As for *The Works of that Eminent and Learned Lawyer, Sir George Mackenzie*, this book appeared in two volumes over the years 1716–22, and represents something of the remarkable range of an author whom Dryden saluted as 'that noble wit of Scotland', and whose interests included heraldry, poetry, fiction, moral philosophy, and history, as well as law. Watson may have singled him out more for the political reputation that made him 'Bluidy Mackenzie' to the Covenanters than for his legal ability, which made his *Institutions of the Law of Scotland* (1st edn 1684) an authoritative work for generations of Scots lawyers.

As a printer and publisher Watson did much to encourage historical studies in Scotland. Some of his books are polemical and look back to the glories of the national past to teach lessons about contemporary politics of church and state. One example along this line is Alexander Lauder's *Ancient Bishops consider'd; with respect to the extent of their Jurisdiction, and Nature of their Power*. 'In answer to Mr Chillingworth and others. Wherein the Conformity of the government and Discipline of the Church of Scotland, with that of the Ancient Church, is fully manifested'. This book was published in the year of the Union. Of a different nature are the archaeological and historical treatises of Sir Robert Sibbald (1641–1722). Watson printed the first of these, dealing with Roman antiquities in Scotland, in 1707, and followed it three years later with *The History, Ancient and Modern, of the Sheriffdoms of Fife and Kinross.* He then allowed the project to be taken up by Andrew Symson (1638–1712), a printer with execrable standards but with jacobite sympathies who had formerly been an episcopalian clergyman. Symson was also the author of a reasoned argument in verse in favour of the Union: *Unio politico-poetico-joco-seria* (1706). Sibbald's work represents the older style of antiquarian research associated with the names of Dugdale and Camden in England, but his attention to sources and documents anticipated the studies of Lord Hailes later on in the eighteenth century and ultimately the activities of Walter Scott and David Laing in the nineteenth. These men came to have an imaginative and sympathetic view of their country's past lacking in the school of philosophical historians led by David Hume and William Robertson.

Historical works published by Watson which celebrate the House of Stewart and stress its legitimacy are George Crawfurd's *Geneological History of the Royal and Illustrious Family of the Stewarts* (1710) and Sir George Mackenzie's *Historical Account of the Conspiracies by the Earls of Gowry, and Robert Logan of Restalrig against King James VI* (1713). To the latter book was added a 'Vindication of Robert III', the first Stewart king. These and other books of a like kind published about the time of the Union are answers to the denials of Scottish sovereignty by English nationalists such as William Atwood, also to scepticism directed at the alleged antiquity of the Scottish royal line by the English bishops Lloyd (*Historical Account of Church Government,* 1677) and Stillingfleet (*Origines Britannicae,* 1685). Much 'controversial history' was engendered thereby, but the associated research bore fruit gradually in a more scientific attitude to charters, as is manifest in the great production of

James Anderson, *Selectus Diplomatum et Numismatum Scotiae,* printed by Thomas and Walter Ruddiman in 1739, some eleven years after the author's death. A work of literary history published by Watson which promises much in its title but proves disappointing on inspection is Dr George Mackenzie's *Lives and Characters of the most Eminent Writers of the Scots Nation* (1708, 1711, 1722).

Ironically enough, the climax of Watson's career as a publisher of historical works came with the appearance of a monumental book by a presbyterian and whig scholar, who was perhaps the most assiduous researcher and voluminous writer of all the historians of his country: Robert Wodrow's *History of the Sufferings of the Church of Scotland* (1721–2). James Watson died in the year of the publication of the second volume, twenty-seven years after commencing as printer. His press launched the vernacular revival in Scotland, as we have seen, and the record of his publications warrants the patriotic charge to his fellow-printers in the preface to *The History of the Art of Printing:* 'I wish none of you may have your Country's Honour less at Heart as to PRINTING, than I have had it; and spend as much of your Money and Time for reviving PRINTING in this Part of the Island, as I have done' (pp. 23–4).

Less steady in his application to printing and publishing and perhaps more desperate in his politics was Robert Freebairn (d. 1747), whose list of books, however, is impressive and evinces a definite policy of literary patriotism.[11] His father was a non-juring clergyman forced to earn a living after the Revolution as a bookseller, though he died as episcopalian bishop of Edinburgh. The son became a bookseller after his graduation at Edinburgh in 1701, and within three years was a member of the Royal Company of Archers, then a hotbed of jacobitism. Two years later he turned printer, as Watson recounts: 'In 1706, Mr John Spotiswood Advocate, and Professor of Law, bought a neat little House for printing his Law Books: But in a little time after, dispos'd of it to Mr Robert Freebairn Bookseller, who has very much enlarg'd the same, and done several large Works in it' *(History of the Art of Printing,* preface, pp.

18–19). Freebairn had aspirations to being a scholar-printer, but his rival in business and temporary suborner, Mrs Anderson, reckoned he was more learned in the school of Bacchus than in those of grammer and typography.[12]

His first publication was Henry Maule's *History of the Picts* (1706), which Freebairn thought of as a contribution to the writing of a new national history, a project much canvassed at this period. His next important book from our point of view was an edition of the Ciceronian dialogue *De Animi Tranquillitate* by Florence Wilson (c. 1504–51), first published at Lyons in 1543. Wilson refers to the threat of war between England and Scotland and reasons that strife will cease when the two countries are one. These sentiments were appropriate for 1707, when even a jacobite such as Freebairn could endorse the idea of Union. Patriotism is represented by Wilson's expression of love for Scotland and his elegant description of his birthplace near Elgin cathedral. Another work of Scottish humanism issued by Freebairn was Arthur Johnston's *Cantici Solomonis Paraphrasis* (1709), with the dedication, preface, text, and notes all by Thomas Ruddiman.

That same hand was responsible for the considerable textual and linguistic efforts expended on the translation of the *Aeneid* 'into Scottish verse' by Gavin Douglas, which Freebairn published in 1710 with the help of Andrew Symson. It would be tempting to consider this folio volume as a triumphant expression of Scottish pride in a master work of the national literary heritage, particularly in view of the ancillary parts suggestive of the treatment afforded classical works. However, in the preface and elsewhere Freebairn and Ruddiman refer to Douglas's language as 'primitive', 'incorrect', and 'licentious'. Latin is the standard against which other languages are measured, and though recognition is given to the unique expressiveness of Douglas's Scots, it is clearly held to come a long way behind the classical tongue.

The preface suggests that the original thrust for the edition came from Dr Archibald Pitcairne (1652–1713), medical scientist, Latin poet of distinction, and jacobite satirist, one of the leading intellectuals of his time, to whom

Ruddiman owed his start in Edinburgh. Pitcairne's interests are probably to be understood in terms of a desire to further Latin studies and to arrive at the meaning of Douglas's Scots. It is thought that Sir Robert Sibbald, also a patron of the edition, was the agent for transmitting to the editors the views of English scholars about the need to collate texts and add a glossary. Sibbald's English contacts included William Nicolson, author of *The Scottish Historical Library* (1702), and John Urry, editor of *The Works of Chaucer* posthumously published in 1721.[13]

The result was a text based on William Copland's anglicised version, *The xiii. Bukes of Eneados of the famose Poete Virgill Translatet out of Latyne verses into Scottish metir* (London 1553). Rather late in the history of the Freebairn-Ruddiman edition, this earliest printed text of Copland's was corrected against the Ruthven MS in Edinburgh University Library. Ruddiman also added the 'Large Glossary, Explaining the Difficult Words. Which may serve for a Dictionary to the old Scottish Language', an addition which Freebairn's preface affirms was 'earnestly desired by many ingenious Men both here and in England, yet was neither at first design'd nor promis'd by us', and which apparently delayed the publication of the book. The compiler was an excellent Latinist but had scanty resources in the 'Ancient Northern Languages', and he drew sparingly on the older Scottish authors. Ruddiman had a good Scots tongue in his head, however, and he had access to Scots speakers from different regions: 'It was found necessary also to converse with People of the several Shires and Places, where some of the old Words are as yet used. This seemed the best Method for discovering their true Meaning, next to the Comparing of Translations with the Originals; for tho the Vulgar are not able to give the Etymology of a Word, or any Reason why it signifies so, yet they cannot be ignorant what Idea they Express by it: Whereas the greatest Scholars are apt to be mistaken about the Origine, and consequently the Sense of Words' (Preface). Because of these efforts, the edition and its glossary remain one of the most influential works in the eighteenth century vernacular revival. Ramsay used the glossary as the basis of the one he supplied for *The Ever Green,* his anthology of older Scottish poetry, and a century later it was still one of the important sources for John Jamieson's *Etymological Dictionary of the Scottish Language* (1808). Traces of the book's influence appear in all the major poets of the century: in Ramsay's adoption of the pseudonym 'Gavin Douglas' as a member of the Easy Club; in Fergusson's proposal for a complementary translation of the *Eclogues* and *Georgics;* and in Burns's choice of a motto from it at the head of 'Tam o' Shanter'.

A year after the appearance of Douglas's *Aeneid,* Freebairn turned his attention to the daunting task of publishing the *Opera Omnia* of the great humanist George Buchanan. Perhaps his publication (1708) of a commentary on Buchanan's *History of Scotland* was a preparation for the more ambitious enterprise of the complete works. Printing began in 1713 and was completed in 1715, though the book was not generally released to the booksellers until Freebairn returned to Edinburgh in 1722 following his escapades during the jacobite rising of 1715 and its aftermath. The learned preface which appears over Freebairn's name and the extensive *apparatus criticus* can be attributed to Thomas Ruddiman. It is a measure of Freebairn's confidence in the work as meeting a national demand that he published it as open stock rather than by subscription. Ten years later, Buchanan's European reputation as a Latinist still warranted the edition of the *Opera Omnia* being reprinted at Leyden by Peter Burman (1725).

In connection with editions of Scottish authors it has been claimed that about 1715 Freebairn printed a black-letter text of Blind Harry's *Wallace* in a modern edition which shows some signs of collation with the unique manuscript of 1488 now in the National Library of Scotland. This edition was finally published at Edinburgh with the date 1758 on the title page and no identification of the printer. There is a companion edition of Barbour's *Bruce.*[14] On the fly-leaf of a copy of the 1758 *Wallace* in the Edinburgh Central City Library, there is written a note to the following effect: 'This Edition of Wallace was printed in or before 1715 for the purpose of stirring up the Scotts — it was then suppressed and was found 30 or 40 years after in a Garret in the Canongate. The title had either never been printed or was cancelled for all the copies have modern title pages'.

On the history side, Freebairn with Ruddiman's help printed in 1711 and 1715 the two bulky and, as it proved, almost unsaleable tomes of Dr Patrick Abercromby's *Martial Atchievements of the Scots Nation*. In September 1715, Freebairn aimed at 'martial achievements' himself by taking part in a jacobite plot to capture Edinburgh Castle. In the same month, there came from his press the declaration of the Earl of Mar setting forth the ills of Scotland and how James III would remedy them. Freebairn then fled to Perth to escape Hanoverian retribution, and subsequently operated a printing press for the insurgents, using equipment commandeered from Aberdeen. After Sheriffmuir he accompanied the jacobite army on its retreat northwards, then went to the Continent where he acted as a courier and emissary among the leading Scottish exiles and apparently sold books. He was back in Edinburgh for certain by 1722 and quietly resumed his former title as King's Printer, being co-partner with the Englishman Baskett.

From the later stages of Freebairn's career, which was beset with disappointments and petty troubles that pushed him to the verge of bankruptcy, there remain two works important for the national literary heritage: Robert Lindesay of Pitscottie's vernacular *History of Scotland* (1728), and John Major's *Historia Majoris Britanniae, tam Angliae quam Scotiae* (1740). It is a remarkable tribute to this adventurous man, Robert Freebairn, that in his Douglas he printed the finest piece of translation by a Scottish poet; in his Buchanan, the work of the greatest Scottish humanist; in his Lindesay of Pitscottie, the nation's foremost vernacular historian; and in his Major, the work with the widest appeal by the last of the schoolmen.

Inevitably in an account of the patriotic publishing enterprises of James Watson and Robert Freebairn, mention has had to be made of Thomas Ruddiman (1674—1757).[15] Hailing from the largely episcopalian north-east and the protégé of Dr Pitcairne, his politics like those of Watson and Freebairn were nationalist and jacobite. As the premier Latin scholar and textual critic of his time, and readily accessible as Under-Keeper of the Advocates' Library, where he presided over extensive legal and historical collections that embraced a variety of disciplines, he was drawn into those publishing ventures, already described, which exhibited to contemporaries something of the achievements of Scottish authors. Ruddiman's particular bias was the defence and advancement of the high standard of Latinity which was Scotland's inheritance from the Renaissance, as is attested by his highly successful *Rudiments of the Latin Tongue* (1st edn 1714), and his more advanced *Grammaticae Latinae Institutiones*, the first volume of which appeared in 1725.

In addition to his careers as scholar and librarian, Thomas Ruddiman from 1712 on was involved with his brother Walter in running a printing house, which at first was a subsidiary of that of Freebairn. Thomas was the business director and corrector of the press, while Walter was the tradesman. The Ruddiman press is celebrated now for printing the works of Allan Ramsay, the first widely-known and popularly-acclaimed poet of the Scottish vernacular revival. Thus, the Ruddiman imprint is borne on the following first editions of Ramsay's productions: *Poems* (1721); *The Ever Green* (1724); *The Tea-Table Miscellany* (1724); and *The Gentle Shepherd* (1725). It is likely, also, that the Ruddimans printed Ramsay's first broadsides: the *Elegy on Maggy Johnson* (?1713); *A Poem to the Memory of the Famous Archibald Pitcairne, M.D.* (1713); *On this Great Eclipse* (1715), and so on. Ramsay was a good investment as an author but his printers served him badly, as his comment on the 1728 edition of *The Gentle Shepherd* makes clear; 'This edition has too many capitals at the beginning of words and is, in many respects, inelegantly printed'. Accuracy rather than elegance was, in fact, the Ruddiman watchword, but it is also likely that Thomas Ruddiman did not consider Ramsay's literary activities worth the dignified treatment accorded the Latin classical authors issued by his press. Towards the end of his career, Ramsay had his poems issued by the Foulis press in Glasgow.

The Ruddimans had no policy such as that adopted by Freebairn in the pre-1715 stage of his career to publish great works of the national literature. Rather they provided the staples of a Scottish scholarly press: school text-books, legal works, and scientific and medical treatises, also works of an historical or antiquarian cast often written from a tory viewpoint. Among the more important works in the last category are the following: *Epistolae Jacobi Quarti, Jacobi Quinti, et Mariae, Regum Scotorum*, ed. Ruddiman (1722—4) — still not superseded as a source for sixteenth century Scottish history; Robert Keith, *The History of the Affairs of Church and State in Scotland, from the Beginning of the Reformation . . . to the Retreat of Queen Mary into England* (1734) — valuable for its original documents; Keith's *A Large new Catalogue of the Bishops of Scotland, down to the Year 1688* (1755); and James Anderson, *Selectus Diplomatum et Numismatum Scotiae Thesaurus* (1739), for which Ruddiman supplied the learned introduction and notes, besides solving with considerable skill the vexing problems of printing the numerous illustrations from the beautiful engravings by John Stuart. The veteran controversialist's last published book was a fitting coda to an heroic career of devotion to patriotic scholarship: *Audi Alteram Partem; or a further Vindication of Mr Thomas Ruddiman's Edition of the great Buchanan's Works* (1755).

There remains now the task of giving an account of the publishing activities of Allan Ramsay (1684/85—1758) to the extent that they manifest patriotism and make clear his position in the development of the Scottish vernacular revival. Though he possessed little in the way of formal education, Ramsay affirmed in a manuscript 'Life' that as a boy in Lanarkshire he read metrical versions of the lives of Wallace and Bruce (probably deriving from Blind Harry and Barbour), as well as the poems of Sir David Lindsay.[16] Such books would tinge his mind with a patriotic fervour likely to be increased as he lived in Edinburgh through the political events of the first decade of the eighteenth century. His first attempts at poetry were in the fashionable modes of the school of Pope, but possibly through membership of the Easy Club, 1712–15, nationalist feeling took over, and about 1718 Ramsay began to demonstrate great interest in the native literary tradition by publishing broadside editions of 'Christis Kirk on the Grene' to which he added new cantos of his own. These reveal his strengths and weaknesses as a poet — cleverness at pastiche, good control of the vernacular, a degree of spiritedness in conception, and a streak of vulgarity or uncertainty of taste that sometimes results in weak lines and desperate rhymes. Also in 1718, Ramsay published a number of other poems that show a creative response to other models to be found in Watson's *Choice Collection,* the mock-elegy and 'last dying word' poems by Sempill and Hamilton of Gilbertfield. Ramsay drew on his knowledge of Edinburgh low life to produce the highly successful mock-elegies on Maggy Johnson and Lucky Wood, which modulate agreeably from lament to the theme of boon companionship, and 'Lucky Spence's Last Advice' — grim and ironical advice from an old bawd to new ones on the game, the tone somewhat marred in the accompanying notes by Ramsay's coy approach to obscenity. These poems are in the 'standart Habby' stanza, which Ramsay also used in an exchange of verse epistles with Hamilton of Gilbertfield. Here Ramsay pays tribute to the older poet's example, and shows his awareness of the historical scope of Scottish poetry:

> The Chiels of *London, Cam,* and *Ox,*
> Ha'e rais'd up great Poetick Stocks
> Of *Rapes,* of *Buckets, Sarks* and *Locks,*
> While we neglect
> To shaw their betters. This provokes
> Me to reflect
> On the lear'd Days of *Gawn Dunkell,*
> Our Country then a Tale cou'd tell,
> *Europe* had nane mair snack and snell
> At Verse or Prose;
> Our Kings were Poets too themsell,
> Bauld and Jocose.[17]

Ramsay clearly accepts Douglas as important in the history of Scottish vernacular poetry and, unlike Freebairn and Ruddiman, has no bias in favour of the superior status of Latin studies. His verse epistle to Hamilton also suggests that the Scottish literary tradition has been neglected in favour of the English one and that this matter should be put right. In the preface to the 1721 edition of his poems, Ramsay declares that he has no pretensions to being a classical scholar and adds that eminent men of letters have told him that this is no disadvantage, their advice being: 'Pursue your natural Manner, and be an original'. Also in this preface, Ramsay champions ardently the expressiveness of Scots, though he shows some deference to the genteel taste that might take objection to his 'Scotticisms'. It is an historical fact that Ramsay's mixture of assertive and apologetic attitudes about Scots was reflected in other poets of the vernacular revival, most notably by Burns, who veered from representing himself as a 'primitive' — the 'Heaven-taught ploughman' — to claiming his position as a national bard with a long tradition behind him.

Like Watson in being anti-English, as can be seen from his poems 'Tartana: Or, The Plaid' and 'The Three Bonnets', and like Freebairn in being a jacobite, though of the 'soft' variety that contented itself with sentimental indulgence rather than political action, Ramsay followed their lead in patriotic publishing by becoming the editor of two important collections of Scottish poetry: *The Tea-Table Miscellany* (i, 1724; ii, 1726; iii, ?1727; iv, 1737; 10th edn '4 parts in 1 vol.', 1740); and *The Ever Green*, 'being a Collection of Scots Poems, wrote by the Ingenious before 1600' (1724). *The Tea-Table Miscellany,* like Ramsay's own poems, had an instantaneous and widespread success, as the publishing history shows. The attraction was Ramsay's display of something of the wealth of Scottish songs. While his versions may have established anaemic, anglicised wording in place of the original Scots, they probably kept alive tunes that would otherwise have been lost. It is true, however, that the *Miscellany* included only the names of the tunes, not the music, though this was remedied in part in 1726 when there appeared under Ramsay's own imprint *Musick for Allan Ramsay's Collection of Scots Songs,* with settings by

113

Alexander Stuart. Some of the *Miscellany's* riches are suggested by the following titles: 'Todlen Hame', 'Rare Willy drown'd in Yarrow', 'Bonny Barbara Allen', 'Johnny Faa, the Gypsy Laddie', 'The Bonny Earl of Murray', and 'Waly, waly, gin love be bonny' —

> When we came in by Glasgow Town,
> We were a comely Sight to see;
> My Love was cled in the black Velvet,
> And I my sell in Cramasie.

When it is remembered that Watson's *Choice Collection* was weakest in songs and had none of the ballads of Scotland, the significance of Ramsay's work is seen in its true perspective. The remarkable success of *The Tea-Table Miscellany* helped to promote the continuous interest in Scottish songs throughout the century, culminating in the extensive collections of David Herd (published in part, 1769 and 1776) and the work of Robert Burns as songwriter for James Johnston's *Scots Musical Museum* (1787—1803) and George Thompson's *Select Collection of Original Scottish Airs* (1793—1818).

While in no way seen to advantage as the editor of *The Ever Green,* Ramsay deserves credit for being conspicuous enough as a proponent of national literature to secure the use of the Bannatyne Manuscript, the chief source of so much of the older Scottish poetry. The manuscript came into the possession of the Hon. William Carmichaell in 1712 by gift from a descendant of the son-in-law of the compiler, and in 1772 it was presented to the Advocates' Library. The almost equally important Maitland Folio and Quarto Manuscripts lay unknown in the library of Magdalene College, Cambridge, in the Pepys Collection until Bishop Percy brought them to the attention of John Pinkerton, who published their contents in 1786.

In the preface to *The Ever Green,* Ramsay expressed the patriotic ideals behind the publication and adopted a positive tone that contrasts pleasingly with the defensiveness of Watson's introduction to the *Choice Collection:* 'When these good old *Bards* wrote, we had not yet made Use of imported Trimmings upon our Cloaths, nor of foreign Embroidery in our Writings. Their *Poetry* is the Product of their own Country, not pilfered and spoiled in the Transportation from abroad: Their *Images* are native, and their *Landskips* domestick; copied from those Fields and Meadows we every Day behold. The *Morning* rises (in the Poets Description) as she does in the *Scottish* Horizon. We are not carried to *Greece* or *Italy* for a Shade, a Stream or a Breeze. The *Groves* rise in our own Valleys; the *Rivers* flow from our own Fountains, and the *Winds* blow upon our own Hills' (pp. vi–vii). Noble sentiments! though not exactly true in the case of William Dunbar, whose May mornings and gardens of love are highly traditional, literary, and cosmopolitan. Still, *The Ever Green* recovered from oblivion a substantial part of the poetry of Henryson, Dunbar, and Alexander Scott; as well as an older text of 'Christis Kirk on the Grene' (which Ramsay follows Watson in presenting as the opening poem of his selection); a sampling of *The Gude and Godlie Ballatis*; and a text of *The Cherrie and the Slae* alleged to come from the editions of 1597 and 1617. The collection also contained Lady Wardlaw's pseudo-ballad 'Hardyknute' and two pastiches by Ramsay himself; 'The Vision' (in the *Cherrie* stanza) and 'The Eagle and the Robin Redbreast', which are vehicles for jacobite and nationalist feelings, prudently but somewhat feebly disguised in antique dress. Ramsay made errors in transcription, mistook the meanings of old Scots words, chopped up stanzas to suit his fancy, added on bits and pieces to the poems (most ludicrously in the case of Dunbar's 'Lament for the Makaris'), ironed out the old metres, substituted words, and censored blasphemy, to provide a veritable chamber of editorial horrors. *The Ever Green,* unlike *The Tea-Table Miscellany,* did not meet with popular approval and was only reprinted once in the eighteenth century (1761). But the scholars took notice. Lord Hailes published a more faithful edition of selected texts from the Bannatyne Manuscript in 1770, adding forty poems to those chosen by Ramsay while omitting on the grounds of obscenity or obscurity some poems found in *The Ever Green.* Not until the nineteenth century were full editions of Dunbar (1834, supplement 1865) and Henryson (1865) made available by David Laing to bring to fruition the patriotic groundwork of Ramsay as editor and publisher of the older Scottish poetry.

On the evidence presented, then, it may be allowed that from 1706 until 1740 there was a recognisable era in Scottish publishing, opened by the appearance of Watson's *Choice Collection* and ended by the printing of the first edition of all four parts of *The Tea-Table Miscellany*, also the year of Ramsay's retirement to his 'Goose-Pie' house on the Castle Hill of Edinburgh. During that era much of Scotland's lost or neglected literature was restored to her. Barbour, Blind Harry, Sir David Lindsay continued to be available; Gavin Douglas's *Aeneid* and the works of Buchanan, Drummond of Hawthornden, and Mackenzie of Rosehaugh were presented to the reading public in scholarly editions. The riches of Scottish songs and ballads were revealed. In *The Ever Green* the significance of such collections as the Bannatyne Manuscript as sources for the work of the old makars was made apparent. Scottish historical writing during this period also received its share of attention, with the publication of the narrative works of John Major, Lindesay of Pitscottie, Robert Keith, and Robert Wodrow, as well as the more technical productions of James Anderson. The printers, publishers, and editors of these works — James Watson, Robert Freebairn, Thomas Ruddiman, and Allan Ramsay — can be represented as sharing a complex of political attitudes in which resentment over the outcome of the Union played a large part. We have every reason to believe that beyond the hope of gain these men were animated by the feeling expressed by Lockhart of Carnwath, that if Scotsmen would reflect on the heroic actions of their ancestors, which included feats of the pen as well as the sword, they would be inspired to recover what was lost by the Union.

There are indications, however, that towards the end of the period we have singled out as the era of patriotic publishing in response to the Union, there was some resistance to the original impetus. As the anecdotalist John Ramsay of Ochtertyre puts it; 'It is well known that between 1723 and 1740, nothing was more in request with the

Edinburgh *literati,* clerical and laical, than metaphysical disquisitions. These were regarded as more pleasant themes than either theological or political controversies, of which, by that time, people were surfeited'.[18] A key figure in this reversal of interest was Henry Home, later Lord Kames, who was raised an episcopalian and a jacobite but became a deist and supported the whigs. Late in life Kames remembered that in the 1720s he belonged to a Club sponsored by Thomas Ruddiman and Bishop Gillane: 'It consisted mostly of Students of divinity. Lord Kames, Ogilvie, and Campell of Succoth went into it to puzzle and make mischief, and they succeeded but too well with many, making them Deists . . . They used to attack Jacobitism too severely to [suit] Mr Thomas Ruddiman, who was no reasoner. Bishop Gullin was a dull man'.[19] Kames was a leader in the Scottish intellectual revolution which gave his country an honoured role in the Enlightenment. Scots speaker all his long life, friend of Allan Ramsay, he wanted to burst free from the old controversies and old controversialists as 'dull'. He accepted the linguistic consequences of the Union and wrote in English. Perhaps like William Robertson in the passage already quoted from the *History of Scotland,* Kames envisioned the progressive evolution of a United Kingdom culture; perhaps like David Hume, he recognised that English would become a world language. Save for a reference to 'Hardyknute', his *Elements of Criticism* (1st edn 1762), the foundation work of literary criticism in modern times, is innocent of any discussion of literature in Scots. When Scottish vernacular poetry surfaced again in the 1770s, with the appearance of the poems of Robert Fergusson in *The Weekly Magazine* conducted by members of the Ruddiman family, Kames and his like apparently ignored it. Kames's successors among the *literati* in the next two decades patronised the genius of Robert Burns, proving incapable of finding any lasting place in their circle for the poet.

In the career of Walter Scott, the heir of the Scottish Enlightenment in his understanding of the processes of history, the national literature of the era of patriotic publishing again flamed into creative influence. There has come down to us the inscription that Scott wrote in his copy of *The Tea-Table Miscellany:* 'This book belonged to my grandfather, Robert Scott, and out of it I was taught Hardiknute by heart before I could read the ballad itself. It was the first poem I ever learnt — the last I shall ever forget'.[20] Here was the seed of the ballad-raids and the later poems and novels that accorded with and climaxed the publications of Watson and Freebairn, Ruddiman and Ramsay, in giving Scotsmen an opportunity to reflect, as Lockhart of Carnwath desired they would, on 'the Glorious and Heroick Actions of their Progenitors'. But just as the genius of Burns in making songs transformed the lust and hypocrisy and love and drunken gaiety experienced in an Ayrshire parish into universal art, so the genius of Scott as a storyteller gave the struggles of the Scottish people a permanent place in the imagination of the world. It would seem, then, that while Lockhart's hopes for the restoration of political freedom to Scotland remained unrealised, the response to the Union of Watson, Freebairn, Ruddiman, and Ramsay, culminating in the achievement of Burns and Scott, ensured their country its unique and independent place in world literature.

NOTES

1. George Lockhart, *Memoirs Concerning the Affairs of Scotland,* 'from Queen Anne's Accession to the Throne, to the Commencement of Union of the Two Kingdoms of Scotland and England in May, 1707', 3rd edn (London 1714), p. vii.
2. *Bruce:* 1665, 1670, 1672, 1737, 1758 [?1715]; *Wallace:* 1661, 1665, 1666, 1673, 1684, 1685, 1690, 1701, 1709, 1713, 1722 (Hamilton of Gilbertfield's version), 1728, 1737, 1758 [?1715]; Lindsay's *Works:* 1665, 1670, 1672, 1683, 1696, 1709, 1712, 1714, 1716, 1720.
3. Smith to William Strahan, 4 April 1760, commenting on Nathaniel Hooke, *The Secret History of Colonel Hooke's Negotiations in Scotland, in Favour of the Pretender; in 1707* (London 1760): facsim. in James Bonar, *Catalogue of Adam Smith's Library*, 2nd edn (London 1932), facing p. xxviii.
4. Henry Grey Graham, *Scottish Men of Letters in the Eighteenth Century* (London 1908), p. 10.

5. See W.J. Couper, 'James Watson, King's Printer', *Scottish Historical Review*, vii (1910), pp. 244–62.

6. Quoted in John Prebble, *The Darien Disaster* (Harmondsworth 1970), p. 18.

7. The Aberdeen Breviary, printed by Chepman 1510 was not acquired by the Advocates' Library until 1742, and the Chepman and Myllar prints (1508) until 1788: see William Beattie, *The Chepman and Myllar Prints: A Facsimile* (Edinburgh 1950), p. xx.

8. Robert Garioch [Sutherland], *Selected Poems* (Edinburgh 1966), p. 15.

9. The discussion here of the *Choice Collection* owes much to David Daiches, 'Eighteenth-Century Vernacular Poetry', in *Scottish Poetry: A Critical Survey*, ed. James Kinsley (London 1955), pp. 150–84, 309–15; see, also John Butt, 'The Revival of Vernacular Scottish Poetry in the Eighteenth Century', in *From Sensibility to Romanticism: Essays Presented to Frederick A. Pottle*, ed. H.W. Hilles and H. Bloom (New York 1965), pp. 219–37.

10. Ian Ross, 'The Form and Matter of *The Cherrie and the Slae*', *Texas Studies in English*, xxxvii (1958), pp. 83–4.

11. W.J. Couper, 'Robert Freebairn: The Pretender's Printer', *Scottish Historical Review*, xv (1918), pp. 106–23, supplemented by Douglas Duncan, *Thomas Ruddiman: A Study in Scottish Scholarship of the Early Eighteenth Century* (Edinburgh 1965), pp. 41–63.

12. *A Brief Reply to the Letter from Edinburgh relating to the Case of Mrs. Anderson. Her Majesty's Printer in Scotland* (Edinburgh ?1712), quoted in Couper, 'Freebairn', p. 107.

13. Duncan, *Ruddiman*, pp. 51–4.

14. William Geddie, *A Bibliography of Middle Scots Poets*, Scottish Text Society [STS] (Edinburgh 1912), p. 144; see, also, [R.O. Dougan], *Catalogue of an Exhibition of 18th-Century Scottish Books at the Signet Library* (Cambridge 1951), p. 35.

15. The account of Ruddiman's career given here draws heavily on Dr Duncan's book already cited; see, also, George Chalmers, *The Life of Thomas Ruddiman* (London 1794).

16. Burns Martin, *Allan Ramsay: A Study of His Life and Works* (Cambridge, Mass. 1931), p. 18.

17. Answer 1, 10 July 1719, *The Works of Allan Ramsay*, ed. Burns Martin and J.W. Oliver (Edinburgh 1945), i, p. 120.

18. John Ramsay of Ochtertyre, *Scotland and Scotsmen in the Eighteenth Century*, ed. A. Allardyce (Edinburgh 1888), i. pp. 195–6.

19. James Boswell, *Private Papers from Malahide Castle*, ed. G. Scott and F.A. Pottle (New York, priv. ptd. 1928–34), xv, p. 284.

20. John Gibson Lockhart, *The Life of Sir Walter Scott, Bart.* (London 1893), p. 23.